GÜNTER FIGAL

Philosophy as Metaphysics

Günter Figal

Philosophy as Metaphysics

The Torino Lectures

Mohr Siebeck

Günter Figal, born 1949; 1976 PhD; 1987 Habilitation; 1989–2002 Professor of Philosophy at the University of Tübingen; 2002–2017 Professor of Philosophy (Chair) at the University of Freiburg im Breisgau.

ISBN 978-3-16-155734-7 / eISBN 978-3-16-157577-8
DOI 10.1628/978-3-16-157577-8

The Deutsche Nationalbibliothek lists this publication in the Deutsche Nationalbibliographie; detailed bibliographic data are available at *http://dnb.dnb.de*.

The book was typeset by Computersatz Staiger in Rottenburg/N. using Minion typeface, printed on non-aging paper by Gulde Druck in Tübingen, and bound by Buchbinderei Nädele in Nehren.

Printed in Germany.

For A.M.E.S. – also beyond metaphysics

Contents

Acknowledgements

This book was written on the basis of lectures given at the University of Torino in fall 2017. The invitation to these lectures gave me an opportunity to rethink and clarify topics I have been working on again and again and also to give an account of my understanding of philosophy in general. First of all I am especially grateful to Maurizio Ferraris who invited me to Torino and who was a wonderful and amicable host. I am also grateful to Tiziana Andina, Elena Casetta and Erica Onnis of *Laboratio di Ontologia* for support in many respects. It is a pleasure to remember *Caffè Fiorio* with its friendly staff for many pleasant and restorative lunch breaks. Steven Crowell read the manuscript and made helpful comments, Sonja Feger and Elizabeth Wener carefully revised it. Nothing would be as it is without the constant dialogue with my wife, Antonia Egel.

I. Before Beginning

The following explorations are not intended as a contribution to the history of philosophy. They are not 'about' philosophy, but rather philosophical, and, as such an attempt of philosophical self-clarification. Investigating constitutive philosophical questions and problems, they seek to find out what philosophy essentially is and thus to explore basic possibilities of philosophizing. According to this program, non-contemporary conceptions of philosophy will not appear as historical, i.e., as something that is, at best, only indirectly relevant for today's philosophical thinking. Whenever such 'past' conceptions are discussed systematically, they belong to contemporary thinking, and their historicity, though not to be neglected, has become accidental. For the systematic importance of philosophical conceptions it is irrelevant whether they were elaborated a few years, a century, or even two thousand years ago.

Discussing philosophical conceptions systematically always requires critical distance to particular philosophies. Philosophizing is incompatible with dogmatism, and accordingly conceptions already established should not be simply adopted, but critically examined. Someone really philosophizing cannot just be a 'Platonist' or an 'Aristotelian', just as little a 'Kantian', 'Hegelian', 'Nietzschean', 'Husserlian', 'Heideggerian' or 'Wittgensteinian'. The conceptions indicated by these names do not even need repeated representation as if they were canonical doctrines. They are sufficiently represented by their inaugurators. Also, such mimetic representation would be difficult, since philosophical conceptions have no definite content that could be devotedly communicated. Though fixed in manuscripts or books, they are too complex for strict repetition. Rather, every attempt to articulate a particular philosophy will be an interpretation and thus a more or less significant modification of its content; interpretations of particular philosophies will always be 'colored' by the interpreter's philosophical capacities and interests. So philosophical conceptions are nothing that could once and for all be described as or like a matter of fact. No particular discussion of a particular philosophy will be able to grasp this philosophy completely, but rather, in case of success, offer a possible version of it.

Interpretations of philosophical conceptions are also challenged by the fact that philosophies are not isolated from each other. Their respective insights, descriptions, and arguments are connected with those of other conceptions in many ways. They are dependent on others, allude or explicitly refer to others, and they do so both in affirmation and objection. Though interpretations may concentrate on one single philosophy, they cannot really avoid becoming involved with others. So they are more or less to discuss particular topics, not only as those of a singular philosophy, but rather as belonging to a philosophical discourse or tradition or even to philosophy in general. Philosophical interpretations of particular philosophies must also always discuss problems not restricted to these philosophies precisely because they are 'philosophical problems'. Particular philosophies more or less open up the very possibility of philosophizing, and accordingly explorations of such philosophies can, and often will, also discover philosophy as such. There is no way to philosophize outside of philosophy as it is already established. Though philosophizing is not necessarily bound to particular philosophies, it cannot avoid taking place within the realm of philosophies that, in its entirety, can be called *the space of philosophy.* Encompassing all particular attempts to philosophize and enabling, but never completely determining them, the space of philosophy allows philosophizing to constantly begin anew, though never absolutely anew.

The philosophical exploration of philosophy elaborated in the following chapters has a special perspective. Its intention is to investigate philosophy *as* metaphysics. This perspective is only justified if philosophy really is as such metaphysical – not necessarily in every respect, but of necessity in such a way that it cannot be understood neglecting its metaphysical character. Accordingly, attempts at the philosophical self-clarification of philosophy are well advised not to ignore this metaphysical character. However, if philosophy is not metaphysical in every respect, such a self-clarification will also have to determine the limits of metaphysics. And so a complex image of philosophy will emerge; an image, however, that, if these introductory considerations are plausible, is appropriate to the complexity of philosophy.

II. How to Philosophize

Reflecting on 'philosophy', one may first discover that the subject matter thus indicated is difficult to discern. Philosophy is manifold. During its more than two-thousand-year long history, many different ways of how to philosophize developed, and, again and again, questions arose that had not formerly come up. Nevertheless, all different kinds of philosophy must have something in common, provided that the name 'philosophy' is not just a name. In this case there would be nothing like philosophy at all.

What makes philosophies philosophical, however, is not easy to determine. As one soon will realize, it cannot be just a peculiar topic. Philosophy shares many of its topics with other intellectual endeavors, for instance with the sciences, the humanities, with law, and religion and art too. Philosophers often do what scholars in other disciplines also do: they articulate what they have experienced, they develop arguments, and, like philologists or theologians, they give interpretations of texts.

What makes philosophy philosophical can neither be defined as a particular style. There is no single philosophical style – there are various styles, differing remarkably from each other. Though many philosophical writings, like Aristotle's, are treatises, not only they are considered philosophical, the lines of a poem by Parmenides or a Platonic dialogue are too. However, philosophical texts are not necessarily neatly elaborated works. As the example of Aristotle shows, they also can be notes for lectures or manuscripts used as a basis for teaching. Neither are Husserl's, Heidegger's, or Wittgenstein's notes and manuscripts any less philosophical than treatises or works with obvious artistic ambition like Plato's dialogues or Nietzsche's collections of aphorisms. However, if writings of such diverse style can be philosophical, they must have something in common that is independent of their respective style.

What may be common to all philosophies might tentatively be called an *intention*, or, more precisely, an intention different from those of poets, scientists, theologians, philologists, or historians. Since philosophy is so varied, such an intention would very likely be realized in many different ways. These variations, however, possibly result from the intention itself; if so, no prescription would exist of how the intention could be realized best. So the different ways of philosophy may indirectly disclose the intention that essentially determines philosophy. Understanding why philosophers disagree about how to philosophize may lead to an understanding of what philosophy as such is about.

In order to further develop these considerations it may be helpful to adopt a distinction put forward by Peter Strawson. In the introduction of his book *Individuals*, Strawson sketches a basic alternative of performing the intention of philosophy. In doing so, however, Strawson introduces a general characteristic of philosophy – the one leading these investigations – speaking not of philosophy, but of "metaphysics." Strawson does so without further explanation, and thus seems to take for granted that philosophy as such is metaphysical. As to this, however, one should not merely follow suit, and so, before discussing Strawson's basic philosophical alternative, it will be helpful to say something about 'metaphysics'.

The term, 'metaphysics' is *prima facie* no clearer than the term 'philosophy', and, taken simply as a word, it is even less significant. Whereas 'philosophy', φιλοσοφία, means 'love of wisdom' as of real and prominent knowledge, the term 'metaphysics' is not as profound in its origins as one might suppose. There is good reason to assume that the word's original meaning was just an editorial one. It goes back to the Greek τὰ μετὰ τὰ φυσικὰ βίβλια. Andronikos of Rhodos is thought to have coined it in the first century before Christ when establishing a collection of Aristotle's writings. Because he had no distinct title for a particular collection of manuscripts, he simply named it after the place he assigned it to in the sequential order of his edition. Being placed after the books on φύσις, nature, the collection received its name from this position. But even if the title does not originally indicate a move 'beyond the physical', it has obviously been tempting to associate it with an inquiry of the supernatural in whatever way already during the time of later Greek philosophy.

Presupposing this emphatic meaning of 'metaphysics', it might be strange to call every philosophy 'metaphysical' and thus include philosophies solely oriented to 'the physical' and, as a consequence, denying or rejecting any 'metaphysical' aspirations. However, in adopting a critical attitude to metaphysics in an emphatic sense, such philosophies would be closely related to it. They cannot avoid discussing 'metaphysical' questions and thus continue the discourse of metaphysical philosophy. Since they are not metaphysical in the emphatic meaning just mentioned, and also since the emphatic meaning of 'metaphysics' might be all too restrictive, it should be more reasonable to use the term 'metaphysics' in a specific though not emphatic way and to reserve it just for the type of philosophy Andronikos could not easily designate in reference to its particular topic – philosophy as articulated in Aristotle's *Metaphysics* and also in philosophical works of similar intention.

Even without a concrete account of the content of Aristotle's papers collected by Andronikos, one may say that without them the tradition of philosophy would not be what it is. Philosophy after Aristotle's *Metaphysics* is more or less dependent on the basic questions and investigations developed in this book. It is to these questions and investigations the book provides with a kind of philosophical standard that as such also determines critical, 'anti-metaphysical' attitudes. Anti-metaphysical conceptions would then not be metaphysical as such – apart from if they were based on implicit and unacknowledged metaphysical presuppositions. They would nevertheless be philosophical only in dependence on the standard of philosophy. Intellectual endeavors without any reference to this standard, however, would not be philosophical at all. Metaphysics cannot be philosophically overcome as Nietzsche and, most prominently and effectively, Heidegger believed. There is no 'post-metaphysical' philosophical thinking, but only philosophical thinking with a more or less affirmative attitude to the metaphysical standard of philosophy. As a consequence, however, it might be more productive not to argue against metaphysics, but rather accept it as the standard of philosophy. Critical discussions of basic metaphysical assumptions are thereby not excluded. Revisions of metaphysics are normal even, having belonged to philosophy almost from its outset. This is confirmed by Strawson's already-mentioned distinction.

Strawson, however, does not discuss the content or subject matter of metaphysics, but rather two different ways in which metaphysical thinking can be performed. He thus indirectly introduces what metaphysics is about. According to Strawson, 'metaphysics' can be "descriptive" or "revisionary,"[1] and, as one may add, it can be so in a more or less radical way. As Strawson writes, descriptive metaphysics attempts "to describe the actual structure of our thought about the world,"[2] and even without knowing what that precisely means, one might immediately think of an example for such a descriptive attitude. As Wittgenstein writes in his *Philosophical Investigations*, philosophy "must not interfere in any way with the actual use of language, so it can in the end only describe it." And, as he adds, philosophy "leaves everything as it is."[3] As author of *Tractatus Logico-Philosophicus*, however, Wittgenstein can also serve as an example for "revisionary" metaphysics – as a kind of philosophy that, according to Strawson, "is concerned to produce a better structure" of our thought about the world. Another example for such an attempt could be Heidegger, who, in

---

[1] Peter F. Strawson, Individuals. An Essay in Descriptive Metaphysics, London 1959.

[2] Strawson, Individuals, 9.

[3] Ludwig Wittgenstein, Philosophical Investigations. The German text with an English translation by G.E.M. Anscombe, P.M.S. Hacker, and Joachim Schulte, 4th revised edition by P.M.S. Hacker and Joachim Schulte, London 2009, 124.

Being and Time, claims a new beginning of philosophy as retrieval of its beginning in Aristotle's thinking. Heidegger radicalizes his claim in his *Contributions to Philosophy*, dreaming of a new and "differently beginning beginning" of philosophy. And in his late essay *The End of Philosophy and the Task of Thinking*, Heidegger states the necessity of overcoming philosophy as such in favor of a new and completely different way of thinking that he just calls "thinking." Thinking understood in this way is an *absolute* revision of philosophy and thus, as Heidegger thinks, no longer philosophical but radically different from philosophy.

With his characterizations of the two versions of metaphysics, Strawson also characterizes metaphysics as such, namely as a description of the structure of our thoughts about the world. This characterization surely needs further clarification. Though its key terms – "structure", "thoughts," "world" – are not unintelligible, they are nevertheless unclear. One may have a vague understanding of what they mean without being able to discern their meaning explicitly.

This, however, is not a disadvantage, but rather something essential for philosophy. As one may easily see, philosophical thinking in general is not at least an attempt to clarify terms like the ones mentioned – terms that are basically intelligible without being clear. A paradigm for this is Augustine's reflection on time in the eleventh book (XI, 14) of his *Confessions*.[4] As Augustine says, he knows what time is so long as no one asks him.

---

[4] AUGUSTINE, Confessionum Libri XIII, Corpus Christianorum Series Latina XXVII, ed. by Lukas Verheijen, Turnholt 1981.

Being asked, however, and attempting to explain his knowledge, his ignorance about it emerges. The nature of all relevant philosophical questions is perhaps such. The particular ignorance described by Augustine is the beginning of philosophizing. The original philosophical impulse consists in realizing that terms taken as familiar prove to be unclear when reflected on. This impulse, however, leads to philosophizing only if one does not let the vagueness of terms intuitively intelligible rest, but rather makes attempts to clarify them.

Accordingly, metaphysics as Strawson understands it would be confronted with the intelligibility and vagueness of the terms 'world' and 'thought'. What is 'the world', what does it mean to have 'thoughts' about the world, and what is the 'structure' of both? As a consequence of Strawson's characterization, these are obviously 'metaphysical' questions, as are all that are of the same kind as Augustine's question concerning time.

However, if Strawson's characterization is correct, then 'metaphysics' is not sufficiently characterized by its questions. Rather, it is decisive that metaphysics can be practiced in two different ways, namely 'descriptive' and 'revisionary'. This alternative, again, very likely results from the particular character of metaphysical questions. They do not, then, prescribe how they are to be answered. The attempt to answer them philosophically or metaphysically must figure out how such answers are possible – either in simple orientation to the world as it can be described and with descriptions that basically rely on the descriptive force of ordinary language, or solely on the basis of the assumption that one has to disclose something that is hidden by the surface of the appearing world and can only be adequately designated in non-ordinary language.

Pursuing these considerations and thus examining Strawson's distinction more closely, one may find that "descriptive" and "revisionary" metaphysics cannot merely be opposites, but rather must have something in common. Indeed, they share the same concern, namely *description*, with their only disagreement being what descriptive attempts of philosophy should rely on – the "actual structure" of thinking or "a better structure", i.e., either on thinking as it is 'natural' and has become familiar, or on a way of thinking that differs more or less radically from the 'actual' one. In any case, metaphysical discourse is an attempt to elucidate our conceptual access to the world and, in order to do this, to find out and to decide which conceptual access to the world can prove to be more appropriate than others. The first attempt at metaphysical thinking would very likely rely mainly on our familiarity with metaphysical topics, with the expectation that a close look at 'natural' knowledge could make explicit what is normally implicitly known, whereas the 'revisionary' way would stress the necessity of going beyond 'natural' knowledge and finding alternative access to the topics in question.

One may well imagine a dispute between representatives of the 'descriptive' and the 'revisionary' way, and will quite easily discover the character of their arguments. It is probable that each will strive to demonstrate its own metaphysical option as the appropriate one. The criterion for such appropriateness is not difficult to discern. The decisive question is which option discloses the world more, or even most, adequately. This, again, is tantamount to which access to the world can be *true*, and not just by chance, but essentially. Metaphysical discourse, then, is motivated by *the question of truth*. The debate between "descriptive" and "revisionary" metaphysicians is basically about the truth or untruth of normal or revised structures of thinking. As a consequence, it is also a debate about which kind of metaphysics is true – a merely or at least mainly descriptive one, or one that intends to establish a new kind of thinking.

This question, however, cannot be easily answered. The respective truth or untruth of a metaphysical conception, whether descriptive or revisionary, is not a matter of empirical verification or falsification. Representatives of a particular metaphysical conception may regard their own conception as being true, whereas representatives of another metaphysical conception may doubt or contest the ones differing from their own. Disagreement of this kind is a very special one: it can only emerge if the question concerning the truth or untruth of metaphysical conceptions cannot rely on an overall understanding of truth. If, in respect of metaphysical questions, empirical verification does not work and no other criterion for truth is self-evident, then in metaphysical debates the understanding of truth as such is at stake. Accordingly, metaphysical conceptions must include, and at least to a certain degree reflect, a more or less elaborate conception of truth. As it seems, this is what makes them 'metaphysical'. If this assumption is plausible, philosophy being oriented to truth will of necessity be 'metaphysical' in whichever way. It will not necessarily be metaphysical in every respect, and, accordingly, philosophy as such could very likely not be identified with metaphysics. But philosophy that reflects truth will be essentially metaphysical in character.

These considerations can be confirmed by the observation that prominent philosophers, especially in the very early days of philosophy, discussed the problem of truth extensively, and not just as one problem among others, but as the initial question of philosophy itself. There is much evidence for the fact that philosophy originated from the discovery that truth is within reach, though exclusively or at least mainly for philosophy and not for every kind of experience and thinking. By doubting 'ordinary' kinds of experience and thinking, philosophy begins with revisions.

A first example for this – and one for an especially rigid position – is Parmenides. In the introductory part of his poem he imagines a journey on the "far-famed road" on which he has been placed by divine beings (δαίμονες) who also guide his dramatic journey in a cart drawn by horses. The journey takes him to a gate, governed by a goddess, Dike, who is persuaded to open it for him. Inside another goddess, a nameless one, welcomes the voyager, and she does so with a promise. She proclaims that the voyager will "learn all things, both the unshaken heart of the well-rounded truth, and the opinions of mortals, in which there is no true reliance."[5] The promised insight can only be acquired beyond the world normally experienced in human life. One has to become a voyager and leave this world on a path only to be found with the spe-

---

[5] PARMENIDES, VS, B 1, 28–30. Translation quoted from: The Presocratic Philosophers. A Critical History with a Selection of Texts, ed. by G.S. Kirk, J.E. Raven, and M. Schofield, 2nd edition, Cambridge 1983, 243.

cial guidance of divine beings, very likely the daughters of the Sun (Ἡλιάδες) mentioned later in the poem.[6] This path, however, does not lead directly to truth. It is not a path of human insight, but rather one leading to divine revelation.

The truth promised and later revealed by the goddess is absolutely reliable, 'unshaken', and is truth concerning the whole universe; it is 'well-rounded', encompassing everything. It is also the truth about normal human cognition that, if contrasted to divine truth, proves to be just a conglomerate of opinions (δόξαι) none of which, as it seems, will definitely prove to be true or false and thus be part of an indifferent mixture of truth and falseness. Trapped in opinions, one will never understand the difference between falseness and truth, so that the unreliability of opinion can only be understood from beyond. Only from outside the human world and as a divine gift is it possible to distinguish between the unshaken truth of divine insight and the unreliable opinions of mortals. Merely living on the earth and never journeying beyond, mortals are ignorant of the very possibility of the unshaken truth. They remain in the realm of opinions.

Heraclitus holds a quite similar view. As he writes, probably as an introduction to his book *On Nature* (φερὶ φύσεως), i.e., on the essence of all things, normal human beings will be unable to comprehend what he is teaching – "both before they have heard it, and when once they have heard it." They are "like people of no experience, even when they experience such words and deeds as I explain, when I distinguish each thing according to its con-

6 Parmenides, VS, B 1, 9.

stitution and declare how it is."[7] Though Heraclitus, like Parmenides, regards normal human beings rather contemptuously, his statement, compared with Parmenides' poem, marks a clear difference. The thinker himself has acquired understanding and is able to explain his insight so that there is obviously no need of divine revelation. However, one may wonder why Heraclitus bothers to communicate his insight when he is so sure that no one else will understand it. Just in order to demonstrate to normal human beings their intellectual limits? That would be a strange motive for writing a book. Or in order to indicate that no one will easily understand his insights except the few who would be undeterred by his elitist stance and the partly paradoxical character of his thinking? Heraclitus, in any case, seemingly does not wish to encourage or support others in understanding his philosophy.

Plato overcomes Heraclitus' position through a remarkable transformation of the Parmenidean and Heraclitean distinction between privileged insight and normal ignorance. According to the *Republic*, specifically its famous simile of the cave,[8] the way to truth may be difficult, but nevertheless really is one that humans can take – alone and on foot, with neither a horse-drawn cart nor divine guidance. A human being, obviously a philosopher, would free other humans from their bonds and lead them outside the cave that is the normal dwelling-place of humans. Philosophers as such know the way

[7] Heraclitus, VS, B 1. Translation quoted from: Kirk, Raven, and Schofield (eds.), The Presocratic Philosophers, 187.

[8] Plato, The Republic 514a–517c. Quotations are taken from: Platonis Opera, ed. by John Burnet, Oxford 1900–1907.

out. Being 'lovers of the sight of truth' (τῆς ἀλήθειας … φιλοθεάμονες)[9] they must know what they love as well as how and where to find it. Without having experience of truth, one could not love it.

Accordingly, the way to truth as Plato conceives it is no longer an imagined journey. The way out of the cave is not an image of a revelation that cannot be explained in terms of human understanding, but rather of a practicable way of thinking. The image of the cave, however, is a kind of shortcut; a brief story about what can actually become a lifelong venture. Only in philosophical practice this way can adequately be experienced.

Like the Parmenidean experience of truth, philosophical practice in Plato's sense is also to be understood in contrast to unreliable ways of cognition; and as for Parmenides Plato's characterization of unreliability also applies to opinion, δόξα. But the Platonic attitude towards opinion differs radically from the one articulated in Parmenides' philosophical poem. Philosophical practice in Plato's sense does not simply exclude persons sticking to opinions, but rather will include attempts to persuade them of the advantages real philosophical knowledge holds.[10] Philosophical practice is able to guide someone from opinion to true knowledge. The guided must only be willing to follow the argument of the guiding philosopher, who, for his part, must create a chance for the guided to understand. Though from different perspectives, both must be open to understanding and thus

---

[9] Plato, The Republic 475e. Translation quoted from: The Republic of Plato. Translated, with Notes, an Interpretative Essay, and a New Introduction by Allan Bloom, 2nd edition, New York 1991.

[10] Plato, The Republic 476d–e.

take part in common philosophical practice. As a consequence, it is not opinion that is the real obstacle for philosophy, but rather every practice that inhibits understanding. Of such kind are rhetoric and poetry. The goal of rhetoric is persuasion in favor of a speaker's predominance, whereas poetry simply disregards the listener or reader's chance to understand, possibly because poets – as Plato's Socrates suspects in *Apology* – are caught in a kind of divine enthusiasm, and do not really understand what they themselves are saying.[11] According to Plato's *Sophist*, this also applies to thinkers like Parmenides. Every one of these "seems to tell us a story, as if we were children," without taking into account "whether their arguments carry us along with them, or whether we are left behind."[12]

In Platonic philosophical practice, as one may conclude, truth is intelligible, admittedly not for everyone and not in every case, but in principle for all those sufficiently disposed and willing to understand. Truth is not a matter of divine revelation, but of a particular rational discourse that Plato calls dialectics. διαλέγεσθαι means 'to converse' with someone, but also 'to examine and clarify something discursively' and thus find out what it truly is.

For Aristotle, Plato's most ingenious student, the Platonic understanding of philosophy as rational clarification has become self-evident, not to mention the conviction that philosophy as such is devoted to truth. Aristotle

---

[11] Plato, Apology.

[12] Plato, The Sophist 242c, 243a–b. Translation quoted from: Plato, Theaetetus, Sophist, with an English Translation by Harold North Fowler, Cambridge Mass./London 1921.

confirms what Plato would have said, namely that philosophy is the contemplation of truth, ἡ περὶ τῆς ἀληθείας θεωρία, and that it can justly be called the knowledge of truth, ἐπιστήμη τῆς ἀλήθειας.[13] Nonetheless, Aristotle's view on philosophy differs from Plato's. Aristotle does not take philosophy as to be just one, but in line with philosophers today, as a manifold of different philosophical approaches and conceptions. Accordingly, the general characterization of philosophy as knowledge of truth applies to all these philosophies, provided that they really are philosophies. As Aristotle says, no philosophy can completely miss truth, so that every philosopher so far has contributed to a philosophical subject matter, and even if only in a small, particular way, it proves to be something great when gathered to a whole.[14] So as a philosopher one should be grateful to all other philosophers, "not only to those whose views we can share, but also to those who have expressed rather superficial opinions."[15] Such gratefulness which, as it seems, also includes all story-telling thinkers like Parmenides, is especially appropriate since, according to Aristotle, no philosopher can justly claim the capacity to apprehend truth sufficiently.[16] This is obviously not a plea for philosophical revisions, at least not for radical ones. There is no need of philosophical revolutions, since sooner or later every

[13] Aristotle, Metaphysics II.1, 993b 20. Quotations are taken from: Aristotelis Metaphysica, ed. by W. D. Ross, 2 volumes, Oxford 1924.

[14] Aristotle, Metaphysics II.1, 993b 1–4.

[15] Aristotle, Metaphysics II.1, 993b 11–13. Translation quoted from: Aristotle, Metaphysics, Books I–IX, with an English Translation by Hugh Tredennick, Cambridge Mass./London 1933.

[16] Aristotle, Metaphysics II.1, 993a 31–993b 1.

revolutionary attempt will prove in principle to be of the same kind as all other conceptions of philosophy.

Aristotle instead offers a plea for philosophical liberalism; according to his considerations, no philosophical conception is entitled to claim insight only for itself.

It is in line with this philosophical liberalism that Aristotle does not reserve true knowledge for philosophy. In the *Nicomachean Ethics* he distinguishes five different ways in which the 'soul' – or, to give a translation suitable for the context: 'the human mind' – "achieves truth in affirmation or denial." The Greek word corresponding to this expression is simply ἀληθεύειν, an expression to which the non-existing English verb 'to truth' would be an equivalent.[17] Among these ways of achieving truth are art or technical skill in a broad sense, τέχνη, practical reason, φρόνησις, and also scientific knowledge like mathematics and astronomy, ἐπιστήμη. Philosophy, which Aristotle calls 'wisdom', σοφία, thus understanding it not so much as longing for insight, but as having acquired it, has its particular place in the context of such kinds of knowledge. So philosophical clarifications are not isolated from other human endeavors, but rather can rely and build on well-established cultures of knowledge. Philosophy is thus a project well founded in human nature, since, as Aristotle says, all human beings naturally strive to know, πάντες ἄνθρωποι τοῦ εἰδέναι ὀρέγονται φύσει.[18] Situated amidst the intellectual human world, philosophical clarifications can paradigmatically refer to

---

[17] Aristotle, Nicomachean Ethics VI.3, 1139b 15. Translation quoted from: Aristotle, The Nicomachean Ethics, with an English Translation by H. Rackham, Cambridge Mass./London 1926.

[18] Aristotle, Metaphysics I.1, 980a 1.

other kinds of knowledge in order to clarify the essence of truth. Whereas Parmenides, Heraclitus, and Plato argue for a philosophy revising, to quote Strawson again, the "actual structure of our thought about the world," Aristotle is the founder of descriptive metaphysics.

Nevertheless, Aristotle would not deny the very special character of philosophy as discovered by Parmenides and Heraclitus and subsequently elaborated by Plato. Philosophy may use, for example, technical skill as a paradigm for knowledge and truth – as Socrates did in Plato's dialogues – but *as* philosophy it is not technical skill, just as it is not science or practical reason. Philosophical descriptions of knowledge thus differ from reflections immanent to a particular kind of knowledge. They transcend non-philosophical knowledge in order to reveal its structure, and as a result cannot simply affirm the language of the described knowledge. Philosophy as Aristotle practices it transcends ordinary language. So it is Aristotle, and not Plato, who coins expressions that, from an ordinary Greek language point of view, would have sounded strange. For a Greek listener or reader they must have been like the terminology of Heidegger's *Being and Time* for a normal speaker of German; and not by chance did Heidegger model his terms on Aristotle's terminology. With his philosophical terminology, Aristotle demonstrated that philosophy, though being essentially descriptive, cannot do without revisions.

Philosophy in Aristotle's sense, however, does not claim to replace the knowledge it describes in a way such as philosophical insight, according to the simile of the cave, replaces the ignorance of normal human life. Aristotle clearly recognizes non-philosophical knowledge as legitimate, and only in this regard does he claim an insight that is not to be achieved within kinds of knowledge other than philosophy. Such kinds of knowledge may reflect their own possibilities and limits; they may, at least to a certain extent, even clarify the conditions under which their achievements can be true. Philosophy alone, however, will find reflective descriptions of knowledge that are not bound to the presuppositions essential for this knowledge. This, again, is so because philosophy does not only strive toward true insights, but also and essentially devotes its clarifications to the question of truth itself. Thus it can be the 'contemplation of truth' and the 'knowledge of truth' as Aristotle understands it.

As for understanding philosophy as devotion to truth, Plato, Heraclitus and Parmenides would readily agree with Aristotle, as would most other philosophers who came after him. Aristotle paradigmatically articulates the standard of philosophy as metaphysics. Standards, however, often provoke opposition, and as a result, radical doubts and objections have been raised to varying degrees contesting the Aristotelian standard's plausibility. However, such doubts and objections need the standard in order to make their points and thus confirm it. In so doing, they take part in a philosophical discourse that cannot do without the standard commitments of philosophy.

A good example here is Nietzsche, who holds the most prominent position in modern philosophy for making attempts to show that truth is nothing but an illusion.[19] By

---

[19] Friedrich Nietzsche, Ueber Wahrheit und Lüge im aussermoralischen Sinne (1873), KSA 1, 875–897. Nietzsche's works are quoted from: Friedrich Nietzsche, Sämtliche Werke, Kritische

criticizing metaphysics in such a way, Nietzsche in many aspects restates a sophistic position. He takes up arguments against the reliability of knowledge as they conversely function to counter the attempt to demonstrate and affirm the possibility of philosophical knowledge and insight as it is presented in Plato's dialogues, and most clearly and programmatically so in the *Republic*. On the other hand, however, Nietzsche does not understand himself as a sophist. He claims to be a philosopher, and discussing "the philosophers' presuppositions" as he does in the introduction of *Beyond Good and Evil*, he is seeking freedom from presuppositions in a way Plato described as the basic motivation of philosophy.[20] So, one may wonder whether Nietzsche's conception hovering between sophistic positions and Platonic philosophy, can be consistent. In one aspect at least, however, is Nietzsche's bond to philosophy's search for truth beyond doubt. Nietzsche claims the measure of truthfulness for his own thinking, and there are even passages in his writings stating that philosophical inquiry is impossible without the claim of truth.[21] In any case, however, Nietzsche does not overcome philosophy's orientation to truth, and he thus confirms the Aristotelian standard of philosophy.

Nietzsche has not been the only one to problematize the Aristotelian standard. Much the same has been done by representatives of radical skepticism and think-

Studienausgabe (hereafter: KSA), ed. by Giorgio Colli and Mazzino Montinari, Berlin/New York 1980.

[20] Cf. Plato, The Republic 510c–511e.

[21] Bernard Williams, Truth and Truthfulness. An Essay in Genealogy, Princeton/New Jersey/Oxford 2002, 12–19.

ers tackling philosophy as metaphysics from historical or 'deconstructive' perspectives, the latter mostly in dependence on Nietzsche. It is difficult and philosophically unproductive, however, to assess these critical positions all too generally. Only close examinations of a particular position could reveal in which respects such a position would prove to be philosophically productive, partly or even on the whole. This, however, is said from a philosophical point of view and thus led by an understanding of philosophy bound to the Parmenidean-Heraclitean-Platonic-Aristotelian tradition. For such an understanding, a critique of philosophy will be philosophically normal, since philosophy is essentially self-reflective and bound to not only explore the possibilities of insight, but also its own limits. Attempting to think without presuppositions requires attempts to find out whether one's own thinking is determined by presuppositions, and if so, by which. However, such determinations are only problematic if not reflected on, but rather simply 'presupposed'. If critical discussions of philosophy are philosophical, they cannot challenge philosophy as such.

Understanding philosophy according to the traditional standard does not imply that one has to limit oneself to it. As will later be shown, the Aristotelian standard does not apply to philosophy in every respect. Neither must one agree with Aristotle or other philosophers belonging to the standard tradition in every respect. In doing so, one would be inclined to take a philosophical conception as presupposition, and this would not be in line with philosophy's essential independence from presuppositions. Also, the standard of philosophy never has been as homogenous as critical – and simplifying – discussions of 'metaphysics' have suggested. It covers a wide range of manifestations that would all have to be specifically assessed.

The diversity of traditional philosophy applies not at least to the understanding of truth as the basic subject matter of philosophy as metaphysics. There may have been a general consensus about what is at stake with the question of truth, and also a general agreement as to which particular questions should be answered in order to discover and to understand philosophical truth. Philosophers may even have agreed that many, perhaps even most of these questions have been already answered and that many of the answers thus found are true. A consensus of this kind, however, is quite unspecific and easy to obtain. The truth agreed is, as Aristotle says, like a door one cannot miss,[22] and is not something philosophical inquiry has to seek. The particular and not the whole is what motivates and makes philosophical inquiry necessary. According to Aristotle, the specific difficulty for philosophical inquiry is indicated by the fact that one has "some grasp of the whole," but cannot "grasp a particular part."[23] So one may know for sure that philosophy is devoted to truth, but not be able to say in particular how truth is to be conceived. One may have a grasp of the nature of human life without being able to determine what in particular makes human life human. Conversely, one may doubt or even contest particular answers given by philosophers to particular questions without doubting

---

22 Aristotle, Metaphysics II.1, 993b 4–5.

23 Aristotle, Metaphysics II.1, 993b 6–7: τὸ δ ὅλον τι ἔχειν καὶ μέρος μὴ δύνασθαι δηλοῖ τὸ χαλεπὸν αὐτῆς. Translation by H. Tredennick.

or contesting their philosophy as a whole. This, by the way, would be an entirely un-philosophical gesture. Who could seriously state the complete falseness of Plato or Aristotle's philosophy? But one may very well, doubt or contest, for instance, Plato's or Aristotle's characterization of philosophical knowledge or a single detail of this. Since Plato and Aristotle differ from each other in particular conceptions and convictions, both of them cannot be true in every respect. Also, both Plato's and Aristotle's characterizations can be doubted or contested, and accordingly one could be convinced that a better, more appropriate description of philosophical knowledge is necessary and possible.

In the case of such a contest, one would adopt a revisionary stance for Plato's or Aristotle's conception of philosophical knowledge. As it seems, philosophy must, at least partly, be revisionary in order to claim the possibility of appropriate or adequate descriptions or determinations not already established. Original philosophical research is only possible and necessary if not all philosophical questions up to now have been answered definitely and thus once and for all. Whichever way, however, revisionary philosophical claims should be made only in particular. The claim to overcome a whole tradition of philosophy or even philosophy itself in favor of post-philosophical 'thinking' cannot be motivated by philosophically answerable questions. It is more a gesture than an attempt to philosophically clarify a particular topic.

To complement these considerations, one should stress that philosophical investigations belong to a context of philosophical conceptions that is more or less clearly defined, but never determines investigations in every respect. The questions that motivate philosophical inquiry will normally emerge from a particular philosophy or from several philosophies belonging together in a tradition or a discourse on certain philosophical topics. Or, as one may also say, every philosophical question belongs to a certain philosophical *horizon*. In order to answer the question, one will very likely carefully read texts with which the horizon of the question becomes linguistically manifest. One will possibly also assume that other texts could be pertinent to the question and its possible answers. Thus the question's horizon widens. But it will always remain a horizon and thus never include all texts in which philosophical discourse has become manifest. This, however, is advantageous. Without the limits of a horizon, philosophical questions and answers would lose their concreteness, and thus could not be answered at all. They would drown in the vast sea of written philosophical thinking.

Philosophical inquiry does not only and not primarily consist of reading, however. First of all, it must be an understanding of what the texts are about. Only if a philosophical investigator shares a particular subject matter with the text referred to can philosophizing be real investigation and as such be devoted to something objective, something that is a matter of fact in life and world. Plato and Aristotle, for instance, did not invent the different kinds of knowledge they speak about. Rather, knowledge, for example technical skill or practical reason, exists, just as human beings exist as beings possessing and practicing such knowledge.

Like everything, real knowledge and also its correlates can be described in many versions that differ from each other. However, in order to be understood as different versions they must have the same subject matter in common. Being devoted to its subject matter, every description of a certain quality may contribute to understanding a subject matter in question.

Nevertheless, not all such descriptions share the same status. They are more or less effective, more or less convincing, while some are especially distinguished as being '*canonical*'. The latter descriptions should be taken into account by every pertinent descriptive attempt because all other descriptions are more or less based on them. They founded and have never ceased to dominate the discourse on their particular subject matter.

Many such canonical descriptions can be found in classical Greek philosophy texts, and they mostly belong to the writings of Plato and Aristotle. Their importance, however, is not that of a philosophical beginning – as if all later philosophy *per se* must be unoriginal and derivative. This – particularly Heideggerian – assumption overestimates beginnings and ignores the fact that philosophy renews itself constantly with each worthy contribution to the understanding of philosophical subject matters. The texts of classical Greek philosophy are of particular importance simply because they are largely indispensable for inquiries that are to become philosophically state-of-the-art. The more philosophical inquiries are devoted to 'basic' philosophical questions, the more they ought to take the texts of classical Greek philosophy into account.

This does not mean, however, that one should confine oneself to interpreting classical or canonical texts. Interpretation is surely an integral part of philosophy because philosophical thinking, in not pretending to reinvent the wheel, finds itself situated in the context of philosophy that mostly is accessible only in texts. But, as already said, what makes philosophy philosophical is not the interpretation of philosophical texts, but rather its devotion to subject matters. Accordingly, philosophical interpretation should be subordinate to factual clarification for which more than interpretative skill is required. One must instead rely on one's own experiences and find one's own words. For this one should learn to be attentive to language, especially how an expression of philosophical relevance is used in ordinary language. How, for instance, do we use an expression like 'truth'? For philosophical investigations, natural language is all-important because no one can invent a new language. Coining new terms never transcends the space of natural language.

Nevertheless, the question of how an expression is normally used in philosophy is not primarily aimed at expressions belonging to particular natural languages. Asking philosophically how, for instance, the expression 'truth' is used, one is not primarily interested in the meaning of this particular English expression, but rather in the *concept* of truth which can also be linguistically expressed by other words than 'truth', for example by ἀλήθεια, *veritas*, *verità*, *Wahrheit*, and many others. Philosophy is not bound to particular natural languages. Though concepts are only accessible through linguistic expressions, they cannot be reduced to them. The Heideggerian assumption that only Ancient Greek and German are philosophical languages is simply false. Of course one should read Plato and Aristotle, if at all possible, in Greek and Heidegger and Husserl, if possible, in German, and likewise any other philosopher in their native language. However, what, in any case, is philosophically at stake are *concepts*, not linguistic expressions. Concepts transcend particular languages. They can be indicated by different linguistic expressions belonging to different particular languages. For instance, the concept of justice can be made explicit with the word 'justice', but also with 'Gerechtigkeit' or δικαιοσύνη.

Linguistic expressions can function as indicators for a concept because they can be translated into expressions belonging to another language that have the same meaning. Concepts, however, should not be identified with the meaning of linguistic expressions. Not every meaning is conceptual; for instance, a definite article like 'the' has a meaning, a purely functional meaning, which because it does not indicate a subject matter of any kind, is only valid in the context of language. Concepts, on the other hand, are not *per se* restricted to language. Rather, they are determinate possibilities of understanding something that, being conceptually intelligible, must be conceptually determined, not exclusively, but sharing its conceptual determination with other particulars that are determined in the same aspect. The basic operation of conceptual thinking consists of understanding something in a particular determination that really applies to it without assuming that only this can be and be understood in such a way. So concepts transcend not only particular languages, but rather language itself. Concepts are determinate realities that need language in order to become explicit.

Being conceptual thinking that explicates concepts, philosophy is always to be found situated in language as well as in a wholeness of concepts or, as one can also say, in an openness of thinking and conceptual understanding that can be called 'the space of concepts'. This space offers the conceptual potentiality in which thinking can take place in discovering and combining different concepts. In *The Statesman* Plato describes this kind of discovery by comparing it to the art of weaving.[24] Thinking is not bound to particular concepts. It can freely move from concept to concept, but it finds a particular content only if concepts that fit together or even complement each other are combined. One could call such a combination 'a web of concepts' or, since the Latin word for web is *textus*, also a *conceptual text*. Conceptual texts are the fabric of philosophy. They form the particularly philosophical structure of considerations, descriptions, discussions, and interpretations that are articulated in philosophical discourse, either in speech or, what would be necessary at a certain degree of complexity, as a literary text.

The basic description of the situation and character of philosophical investigation just given is meant as a methodological reflection that may help to understand the status of the following considerations. Conversely, these reflections may become clearer with the following discussion of truth as the main topic of philosophy. If philosophy can be justly determined with Parmenides, Plato and Aristotle, and with Aristotle's words, as ἐπιστήμη τῆς ἀλήθειας or, in English, as knowledge of truth, a more concrete philosophical understanding of philosophy would require a determination of truth.

Even with the first steps towards such a determination, one will understand that truth cannot be discussed ex-

[24] Cf. GÜNTER FIGAL, Finding the Right Concepts, in: FIGAL, Freiräume. Phänomenologie und Hermeneutik, Tübingen 2017, 71–81.

clusively. Other concepts will almost immediately come into play, without having been explicitly introduced, but just with some initial and preliminary characterizations of truth. Speaking about truth, such concepts will be *being* and *appearing*. Accordingly, philosophy as devoted to the truth, philosophy as metaphysics, will also be an investigation of being and thus be *ontological*. Philosophy as it is concerned with appearances will also have a *phenomenological* character. With the investigation's progress, more concepts will be taken into account, and many of them will be best articulated in terms of canonical descriptions. A philosophical investigation like the one intended here will not be accomplished easily. Philosophical considerations are principally open-ended, and many of them remain fragmentary. Nevertheless, it makes good sense to develop a coherent argument and to keep its concepts consistent.

III. Truth

The question of how to understand truth can be answered initially in a way already indicated, namely by examining how the word “truth” is used in ordinary language. First, one should note that the abstract noun ‘truth’ can often be reduced to the adjective ‘true’ or the adverb ‘truly’. ‘To tell the truth’ means to say something that is true. This is an utterance, or, more precisely a linguistically articulated proposition or assertion. A proposition or an assertion should not be confused with a sentence. It could be articulated in different sentences belonging to either one language or to different ones, and nevertheless it would be the same proposition. The truth of something said is not necessarily dependent on the words in which it is articulated. One could use other words or translate a true utterance into another language, and it would not lose its truth, provided that different utterances have the same meaning and thus articulate the same assertion.

An assertion, however, is not only to be articulated in a linguistic utterance or in different utterances. It is itself an articulation, namely of a conviction or opinion someone would hold, and mostly not only as long as she or he articulates asserting something. So, if an assertion can be called ‘true’, the conviction or opinion becoming explicit with the assertion must likewise be true. Convictions can be true without being articulated in assertions. Only with articulation, however, can their truth become explicit. As such they can then be communicated and compared with convictions held by others. Forming and confirming, but also revising their respective opinions, persons can locate and advance their respective positions concerning truth. They can also argue in favor of their convictions, further explain them, and seek and find arguments in order to confirm them.

However, not only utterances, assertions, and convictions or opinions can be called 'true'. What can also be true are facts they refer to. In this sense it can be true that it is raining or that Socrates is a philosopher. One could stress the latter by saying that Socrates is 'a true philosopher', not just someone who is called a philosopher or pretends to be one, but rather someone who lived in such a way that his life was a true philosophical life. To show this is one of the main intentions of Plato's dialogues, and in respect to Socrates, they can accordingly be called true if Socrates actually was the true philosopher Plato portrayed him to be.

The truth, for instance, that Socrates is a philosopher and the truth of the opinion and assertion holding this can be schematically distinguished as *objective* and *subjective* truth. These truths – or two sides of truth – are obviously related to each other, but it is not clear from the outset how their relation is to be conceived. According to a view quite common one would say that they 'correspond' to each other. A closer look, however, proves this to be improper. Correspondence is a symmetrical relation, whereas one will soon discover that the truth of the conviction and assertion that Socrates is a philosopher and the truth of the believed and asserted fact are not symmetrically related to each other. While they certainly belong together, they do not simply 'correspond', so that the basic idea of 'correspondence theories of truth' is at best misleading.[25] Socrates may be a true philosopher even if no one is convinced of this, whereas convictions and assertions according to which Socrates is a true philosopher cannot be true unless Socrates is in fact a true philosopher. So the subjective truth of convictions and assertions are *dependent on* the factual, objective truth of something – on the fact that something or someone truly is what he, she, or it is.

On the other hand, however, the factual truth that Socrates is a true philosopher is open to convictions and assertions. It is only *realized* with convictions, and only becomes explicit when asserted and linguistically articulated. In this much, objective and subjective truths are not simply related but *correlated.* Instead of designating their relation as 'correspondence', one can thus call it an *asymmetrical correlation.*

It was Aristotle who first understood and explained truth as an asymmetrical correlation. He argues very clearly for the dependency of the subjective on the objective side, saying that 'you are not white [i.e., wearing a white gown] because we truly believe that you are white, but because you are white we, who say that, say something true'.[26] This is, of course, the exemplification of a general statement that, in Aristotle's terms, holds that the practice of ἀληθεύειν is dependent on a particular true

---

[25] Cf. Richard L. Kirkham, Theories of Truth, Cambridge Mass. 1992.

[26] Aristotle, Metaphysics IX.10, 1051b 6–9: οὐ γὰρ διὰ τὸ ἡμᾶς οἴεσθαι ἀληθῶς σὲ λευκὸν εἶναι εἶ σὺ λευκός, ἀλλὰ διὰ τὸ σὲ εἶναι λευκὸν ἡμεῖς οἱ φάντες τοῦτο ἀληθεύομεν.

being, ὂν ἀληθές.[27] Convictions and statements can only be true *in reference* to something that is truly what it is and, in this sense, *is* true.

The assumption and statement of something true is not just a causal effect of what in fact is true. Those who believe and state something are not stimulated or determined by the believed and stated fact or being to do so. Instead, they could believe and state something different than factual truths. In doing so, persons can fail to believe and state something true and instead believe and state something false, for instance that Socrates is not a philosopher but a sophist. A person could also tell a lie, i.e., know that something is false and voluntarily make a false assertion. Though dependent on a truth that is believed and asserted, true believing and asserting is also a free person's practice and could thus be practiced otherwise. Telling the truth or lying does not just happen. Though someone may be disposed in character to telling the truth or to lying, both are ultimately dependent on a decision.

In believing and asserting, people are mostly not indifferent to what they are referring to. Rather, they *position* themselves to something that, with this positioning, proves to be relevant for them. In doing so, they mostly cannot control or manipulate the factual truth they opine, assert, and speak about. They can only fail to recognize it or make attempts to conceal a factual truth, a 'true being'. Thus, errors and lies confirm the asymmetrical character of the correlation between true facts or beings and true opinions or assertions, particularly in the case of lies. Lies are based on factual truth; someone

---

27 ARISTOTLE, Metaphysics IX.10, 1051b 1.

lying knows more or less clearly what is true, but chooses to neglect it in that same moment.

In order to further determine the asymmetrical correlation of truth, one should examine how the character of truth, both in opinions or assertions and in something that is factually true, can be understood. What, to put it differently, is the 'truth-factor' in opinions and assertions, and what makes something being to be true? Perhaps this question can be more easily answered in respect of opinions and assertions. These can immediately be experienced, so that in order to describe their truth-character one just has to be attentive to how they are performed. So what is the experience of truth in such a performance?

The answer is quite simple. Uttering an assertion and thus articulating a conviction, one has experienced that something is the case, or something is in such and such a way, or just exists. With an assertion, one refers to something that is taken as *being*, whereas with a poetical phrase, for instance, though referring to something, one does not assert that the correlate of reference exists or factually is in a particular way. Accordingly, convictions articulated with assertions are not only cognitive states having a particular content. Rather, they are also *confirmations* of something really being *objectively being there*. Only with such a confirmation does an opinion or an assertion claim to be true. Otherwise it would not be an opinion at all but only an imagination or phantasy. Confirmation, however, is not a gesture in addition to convictions and assertions. Since opinions and assertions as such claim to be true, they must as such be confirmative.

What is confirmed in opinions and assertions is something 'truly being' or, as one can also say, a 'true being'.

Such beings have already been explained as something that really is what it is. If Socrates truly is a philosopher, he *is* a philosopher and not only seeming or pretending to be one. Instead, he is what makes a philosopher a philosopher. This does not mean, however, that Socrates must generally be regarded as a philosopher. But if he truly is one, every opinion and assertion holding that he is not a philosopher cannot be true. So what makes Socrates be true is that he is what he is, namely a philosopher, and what makes opinions and assertions true is their confirmation of what Socrates is.

As a consequence of these considerations, one may assume that the assertion that it is true that something is the case could be equivalent to the simple assertion that something is the case. Aristotle has argued to this effect. As he says, 'the be' and 'the is' signify that something is true, τὸ εἶναι σημαίνει καὶ τὸ ἔστιν ὅτι ἀληθές.[28] This can be illustrated with the emphatic use of the word 'is' already mentioned. By saying that Socrates *is* a philosopher, one could indeed mean the same as the more complicated assertion that it is true that Socrates is a philosopher. Being true then would be truly being, and truly being would be just being.

It should be undisputed that an adequate clarification of truth is not possible without considering being and also that the emphatic use of the expression 'is' can very well indicate that something said is meant to be true. Nevertheless, one should not take for granted that 'being' and 'being true' can simply be identified, so that one could well do without the expression 'true'. Even Aris-

[28] Aristotle, Metaphysics V.7, 1017a 31–35.

totle does not argue for a strict reduction of truth to being, but rather for a particular possibility of using and understanding the verb 'to be'. Used emphatically this verb can indeed indicate the truth of what is asserted. This indication, however, can only be understood if based on an understanding of truth. As Aristotle says, 'the be' and the 'is' can *further*, ἔτι, signify that something is true. In another passage of *Metaphysics*, he mentions being as true being, ὂν ἀληθές, among other meanings of the expression 'being'.[29]

So to recap, though something true must be something that *is*, the notion of truth should not be reduced to the notion of being. One may very well understand what 'being' means and use the expression correctly without indicating a particular truth. One can, for instance, assume that the trees along the street are maple trees without really being sure. One could leave this question undecided and accordingly be willing to revise it as soon as would be reasonable. In this case, the use of the verb 'to be' is without any emphasis. One speaks about something without implicitly or explicitly confirming it being what it is taken to be. This use of 'is' obviously is different from the emphatic use of the expression, which alone would indicate truth.

Why, however, do we use the expression 'is' emphatically? Why do we articulate the already mentioned confirmation of something as 'truly' being with emphasis? An answer to these questions can be given in reference to *situations* in which this confirmation is performed. Emphasizing that something truly is what it is would not be nec-

[29] Aristotle, Metaphysics IX.10, 1051a 34–1051b 2.

essary and reasonable in a case where the stated facts were self-evident. Such emphasis only makes sense if something could be otherwise, and it may be especially motivated if someone else has explicitly referred to it in a way contradicting one's own opinion. In this case, an emphatic use of the verb 'to be' may just be a rhetorical gesture, an attempt to maintain one's own position against a rival one. The emphasis, however, can also be differently motivated. It can indicate someone's interest in how things really are. Such interest, again, would immediately emerge from a basic condition of human life. We live *among* other entities – people, animals, and things, and we are *related to them*, just as they are related to us in different ways. This web of relations essentially forms the world we live in. It more or less explicitly determines us factually and potentially, and accordingly we are and should be interested in exploring these relations and in finding out what entities we are related to truly are. So the emphatic use of the verb 'to be' indicates the natural longing for knowledge that Aristotle mentions in the first sentence of his *Metaphysics*. This, again, ties in with readiness for exploring and discovering what beings truly are.

The relatedness to other beings cannot be reduced to something subjective in such a way that beings would only be what they are in light of our capacity to recognize them. The "world that regards human beings" is not, as Nietzsche says, the world that has been poetically invented by 'us' as the poets of life.[30] It is not the world that only counts as measured by our intentions, interests, and

---

[30] Friedrich Nietzsche, Die fröhliche Wissenschaft, KSA 3, 342–552, here 540, section 301.

preferences and by the evaluations accompanying them. The world that regards us has not been invented by us, but is what it is, and pursuing our intentions and articulating our preferences we have to take its reality into account. What we are concerned with is *objective* being that concerns us in its objectivity.

Neither can this concern – one may call it the 'natural realism' of human life – be reduced to self-relatedness as Heidegger suggests in *Being and Time.* Human life, Heidegger calls it '*Dasein*', is not primarily concerned with its own possibility that functions as a measure of whether or not something is in accordance with this possibility and thus has a meaning and makes sense. Rather, self-concern (*cura sui, Sorge um sich*) is only possible in orientation to an objective world that provides the conditions, possibilities, and limits under which humans can live their lives. In order to be concerned with the question of how to live, we must know these aspects of the world as well at all possible. Self-concern is thus subordinated to knowledge and thereby to finding out how something whatsoever can be discovered and known within the correlation of truth.

If the experience of beings is therefore already guided by the quest for truth in everyday life, then it is very likely that the philosophical question of being does not originate from the initial experience 'that there is something and not nothing' as Heidegger, quoting Leibniz, states at the beginning of his *Introduction to Metaphysics.*[31] Rather, as has been discussed, philosophy emerges from

[31] Martin Heidegger, Einführung in die Metaphysik, Gesamtausgabe (hereafter: GA) vol. 40, ed. by Petra Jaeger, Frankfurt am Main 1983, 3.

the discovery and confidence that true knowledge is possible and that even questions reaching beyond the accustomed realm of experience can truly be answered. According to Aristotle, wonder (θαυμάζειν) is the initial experience of philosophy because it motivates investigation and discovery. With wonder one awakes to explicit ignorance and so becomes able to escape ignorance and find a way to knowledge.[32]

Knowledge as the fulfillment of the quest for truth is related to essentially being – as, conversely, being is to knowledge. As a result, the question of being is originally an *epistemological* question. Pursuing this question, one seeks clarification of how being is to be conceived in its essential relation to knowledge and how it can thus play a part in the correlation of truth. It is, again, Aristotle who most clearly states this. Philosophy, as he understands it, is knowledge of the most knowable, ἐπιστήμη … τοῦ μάλιστα ἐπιστητοῦ.[33] Most knowable are, as Aristotle adds, the first things, and that means the principles – τὰ πρῶτα καὶ τὰ αἰτία. These are, to give an initial and preliminary explanation, the reasons in terms of which both being and the knowledge of being as such is to be conceived. These principles allow philosophical reflection to transcend knowledge devoted to particular beings and thereby clarify the meaning of being as such, whilst also finding a basis for conceiving the truth of being. The principles allow what Aristotle determines to be an exclusive task of philosophy, namely to consider being as

---

[32] Aristotle, Metaphysics I.2, 982b 11–21.
[33] Aristotle, Metaphysics I.2, 982b 1–2.

being and what belongs to being as such – τὸ ὄν ᾗ ὄν καὶ τὰ τούτῳ ὑπάρχοντα καθ' αὑτό.[34]

Aristotle's conception of philosophy or, to be more precise, of theoretical philosophy as a contemplation of being for the sake of truth, is anticipated by Parmenides as well as Plato. Both predetermine Aristotle's understanding of philosophy as devotion to truth as well as his conception of how the truth of being is related to the truth of knowledge. For all three philosophers, it is mainly truth that is at stake, although all maintain that conceiving truth requires a discussion of being. So while philosophy does not originate with the question of being, only with the question of being could philosophy clarify its original concern.

---

[34] ARISTOTLE, Metaphysics IV.1, 1003a 21–22.

IV. Being

The philosophical consideration of being begins with a blank position. Though 'being' is the key term in Parmenides' poem, the author does not make any attempts to clarify what he understands by 'being'. The goddess whose teaching is reported by the poem implicitly even denies that something instructive can be said about being. She only gives a tautological determination according to which "being is" – ἐὸν ἔμμεναι – and the "to be is" – ἔστι γὰρ εἶναι.[35] Slightly more substantial is the information that being must be contrasted to non-being, but since non-being never can be forced to be,[36] the attempt to say more about it is doomed to failure. What can justly be referred to must *be*, and since non-being cannot be, by consequence it cannot be referred to – a conviction that is critically discussed later in Plato's *Sophist*. So non-being is inaccessible, and therefore speaking about becoming or passing, which is essentially contaminated by non-being, is aporetic too. Every change includes non-being – something becoming must 'not have been' before, and something passing by is, or will 'not be' what it has been, or 'not be' at all.

Considering this characterization further, one could assume that something becoming or passing by is ade-

---

[35] Parmenides, VS, B 6.

[36] Parmenides, VS, B 7.

quately understood as a mixture of being and non-being. Parmenides, however, denies the possibility of this assumption. How should such a combination be conceived if non-being is inaccessible? According to the goddess of Parmenides' poem, the idea that being and non-being could be combined is a confusion that dominates the minds of the "mortals" who are "two-headed" – one head oriented to being and the other one to non-being, believing "that to be and not to be are the same and not the same."[37] The 'mortals' speak about non-being, and in doing so they take it for being, but in calling it 'non-being' they at the same time distinguish it from being. As the speech of the goddess suggests, this does not make any sense, even though the 'mortals' obviously take it as doing just that. According to the goddess' speech, only being can be investigated so that only the way oriented to being can be the "path of Persuasion" (πεῖθους … κέλευθος). In contrast, the way of non-being that leads through the world of becoming and passing by, of difference and negation, is not to be investigated.[38]

The goddess' teaching as sketched is quite unsatisfying. It articulates a strong revisionary position without determining its central concept in any substantial way. One could nevertheless argue in favor of this position, stressing that the originality of being cannot be articulated other than in tautologies. According to such an argument, the blank position in the goddess' teaching would not be problematic, but rather do justice to being

[37] Parmenides, VS, B 6. Translation quoted from Kirk, Raven, and Schofield (eds.), The Presocratic Philosophers.

[38] Parmenides, VS, B 2. Translation quoted from Kirk, Raven, and Schofield (eds.), The Presocratic Philosophers.

as such. Then, however, being could not be explained; it could not be the being of something particular with particular properties, since every particular can change and thus would partake in non-being. Being, then, is just being, nothing but being.[39]

Such an apology, however, is not very convincing and accordingly cannot avoid critical questions. If being is just being and immediately experienced as such, how could the 'route to being' be a route of investigation and knowledge? Knowledge must be more than just taking everything as 'being'. Otherwise every immediate impression of something would be knowledge of a true being so that ignorance or error would be impossible. But why, then, should the two-headed mortals be inclined to ignore true being? Why would they assume the existence of becoming and passing, if everything is just what it is, without change and alteration? Is change nothing but an illusion? And how could non-being be inaccessible if one can justly say that something is 'no longer' what it was or 'not yet' what it can be?

Questions like these may have motivated Plato, a fascinated, but nevertheless critical reader of Parmenides' poem, to revise the Parmenidean conception. With his revision, however, Plato does not distance himself completely from Parmenides. In the *Republic*, a dialogue that is especially significant for the discussion of being, Plato rather in principle adopts the Parmenidean view. Admittedly, he does so by portraying the view of Socrates who,

---

[39] In some of his late texts, Heidegger has argued in this way and thus affirmed the Parmenidean position. Cf. GÜNTER FIGAL, Unscheinbarkeit. Der Raum der Phänomenologie, Tübingen 2015, 11–15.

as readers of Plato's dialogues should never forget, is not Plato's mouthpiece, but instead an individual philosophical personality holding convictions that Plato does not indicate to share. As the key figure of many Platonic dialogues Socrates is too lively a person as to be only a mask for someone else's convictions. On the other hand, however, there are no indications in the *Republic* that the author distances himself from Socrates' position. Though he revised Socrates' conception in his later dialogues, he may have regarded it as a necessary first step and only retrospectively as preliminary and propaedeutic. Plato's later revisions, however, have not relativized the prominence and efficacy of the conception developed in the *Republic*. Rather, this conception has been regarded as Plato's own canonical conception of being, possibly because in Plato's later dialogues the concept of being is not as prominent and dominating as in the *Republic*. As a consequence, Aristotle, being essentially interested in the question of being, critically refers to it in order to shape his own conception. In so doing, he canonizes the pertinent passages of the *Republic* for the future discourse on being.

As Socrates states in the *Republic*, philosophers as "lovers of the sight of truth"[40] devote themselves entirely to being, and accordingly seek being that is nothing else other than being, without any enclosures of negativity. They do so in favor of knowledge and thus in favor of truth. "That what is entirely" is also the entirely knowable – τὸ μὲν παντελῶς ὂν παντελῶς γνωστόν.[41] It is ab-

[40] Plato, The Republic 475e.
[41] Plato, The Republic 477a. Translation by Allan Bloom.

solutely stable, without change and thus without any aspects of indetermination. It is completely accessible and can therefore be entirely known. It is as such true and guarantees the truth of knowledge.

Though with such considerations Plato's Socrates follows in Parmenides' footsteps, the version of being presented by him is in many respects refined, much more elaborated and definitely improved. For Plato's Socrates, being is not just mere being so that nothing can be said about it except that it is. For Plato's Socrates, being is instead determined. Every true being is an idea (εἶδος) and thus, as some explicative remarks on this expression will show, being is substantiated with an epistemic determination. The expression εἶδος goes back to the verb *εἴδω, 'I see', which in Ancient Greek was only in use in the aorist form, εἶδον. Accordingly, an εἶδος is something to be seen, and, more precisely, the visible shape of someone or something.[42] Seeing for instance a human being, one sees their shape or form silhouetted against its surroundings. This shape is often distinctive. Viewing a person's shape or form, one may immediately know who the person is. So an εἶδος is something that can be recognized immediately. It is something evident, just like Parmenides' being, but, instead of being 'just being', it is something determinate that can be distinguished from something else of the same kind, just like the shape of one particular person from another's.

Using the term εἶδος philosophically, Plato's Socrates implicitly relies on the sketched meaning. Being primar-

---

[42] Cf. HENRY GEORGE LIDDELL/ROBERT SCOTT, A Greek-English Lexicon, Oxford 1951, 482.

ily determined as εἶδος, being is knowable or known. This, however, can also be inverted: if being as such is the intelligible, then only the intelligible *is*. Understanding being as intelligibility, Plato's Socrates understands intelligibility as being.

It is worth noting that being is not normally understood in this way. Normally, being is taken as something that 'really' is there, before one's eyes, and of such a kind are, for the most part, perceivable things or living beings. According to Plato's Socrates, however, such perceivable beings are only 'like' (ὅμοιον) the true beings that ideas are.[43] For example, beautiful things are not truly, only the idea of the beautiful truly is, or, as Plato's Socrates also puts it, 'the beautiful itself'. The being of beautiful things or living beings is dependent on the beautiful itself, without which they never could be beautiful. This, however, does not mean that the idea of the beautiful is just the beauty of a beautiful living being or of a beautiful thing. Rather, living beings or things as such cannot be beautiful. They can only be taken as beautiful because they 'resemble' the beautiful itself. Seeing something taken as beautiful, one feels reminded of the beautiful itself and, in a kind of confusion that may remind of the confusion the two-headed mortals presented in Parmenides' poem undergo, one says the thing beheld is 'beautiful'. This is like calling someone who only resembles Socrates, 'Socrates' because of this resemblance.

The argument outlined will be familiar not only to readers of Plato but likely to all with a rudimentary idea of his philosophy. However, if not just taken as a 'classi-

---

[43] Plato, The Republic 476e.

cal' philosophical doctrine but considered with regard to its plausibility, the argument will seem puzzling. How should something beautiful be 'like' the beautiful itself instead of just being beautiful? And how is beauty to be experienced if not as the beauty of something perceptible that in its particularity is beautiful?

Socrates' argument may become clearer with his general explanations of how the intelligible determinateness of living beings and things should be conceived. Socrates seeks to strictly distinguish this determinateness from determinate things and living beings, and in order to do this he stresses the essential ambiguity of everything perceivable. According to his explanation, something beautiful is not simply beautiful, but would always also appear as ugly, as would something just as unjust and something holy as unholy.[44] Everything perceivable is therefore *imperfect* since it cannot entirely and completely fulfill a determination and is thus not plainly determinate. Whereas the beauty of something perceivable will always be impaired in one or the other way, only 'the beautiful itself' is supposed to be entirely beautiful. With this conclusion, the Parmenidean tautology is back. It has only been transmitted from pure being to the particular determinateness of an idea as being.

This Socratic version of the tautology is more difficult to understand than the original Parmenidean one. As to the Parmenidean version, one may say with some plausibility that being as such cannot be explained further, but is only what it is – just being. Though this is not very informative, neither is it paradoxical. However,

---

44 Plato, The Republic 479a.

taking beauty as a determinate quality, it seems strange to ascribe this quality to the quality itself, and to stress that only to a quality an identical quality can truly be ascribed. On the other hand, however, Socrates' characterization of perceivable things is not completely inadequate. The assumption should be plausible that something determinate does not necessarily, and thus at least not in every case, fulfill its determination in every respect. Though designating something beautiful as ugly too may sound harsh, one would very likely admit that something beautiful may have less beautiful aspects, weak points as it were, that impair its beauty or may even create doubt whether such a thing could be called 'beautiful' at all. Perceivable things are and even must be determinate – otherwise they could not be understood as something particular with particular properties. But their determinacy can be incomplete. They may fall short of the determinacy they could have in different respects.

Socrates' point, however, is not only that a living being or thing is only partially determined in several or even many respects, but even more that their partial indeterminacy makes them dependent on the views of persons experiencing them. So not everyone will call the same thing 'beautiful', but possibly 'ugly', and this is, *nota bene*, not only a question of personal taste, but rather due to the object's partial indeterminacy. The object is not as distinct as to rule out varying or even opposing views on it. To this effect, Socrates also points out that, for instance, something double may in other respects be called 'half', something big 'small', or something light 'heavy'.[45]

---

[45] Plato, The Republic 479b.

These determinations are not random – as if something experienced as heavy would not really be heavy for the experiencing person. But such determinations apply to something only under certain conditions of experience and thus only *perspectively.* Instead of belonging to something as stable properties, perspective-dependent determinations are only revealed in the interrelation between experiencing persons and their objects of experience. With a change of perspective the determination of something will likewise change.

In this manner, Plato's Socrates understands something partially indeterminate as an *appearance.* Something that appears for instance as heavy to someone less strong will appear as light to someone else who is stronger. Something appearing as divided into two parts can also appear as consisting of two halves and also as being one whole when doubled. Appearance in this sense is understood in contrast to being. Something appearing is defective because it is not just what it is, but rather is only *for someone in a certain respect* and thus may also appear differently to someone else or even to the same person under different conditions. Being, thus contrasted to appearing, must always be the same as the same and thus independent from particular and varying conditions of accessibility.[46]

Before further discussing Socrates' distinction between being and appearing, it may be helpful to remember that, in comparison with Parmenides' conception, the Socratic – or Platonic – explication of being in contrast to appearing really is an advantage. Whereas Parmenides

---

[46] Cf. PLATO, Phaedo 78c–d.

characterizes the beliefs of the 'mortals' only paradoxically – they take being and non-being to be the same yet not the same – the characterization of appearing as given by Socrates is descriptive and therefore in principal convincing. Appearing, indeed, is perspectival so that something that can only be discovered in a particular perspective is never independent from a particular point of view. So what appears can always appear otherwise. With every appearance it is only partly present, and accordingly it can only be incompletely experienced. With appearances, there are always 'dark sides' of the kind that Husserl calls 'adumbrations' (*Abschattungen*).[47] If innumerable perspectives of something are possible, one can, indeed, say that it is not 'entirely knowable'. It cannot be known in a strict sense, but only be *opined*. Appearances are as such accessible in opinion, δόξα, which is clearness only to a certain degree. It is, as Socrates says, "darker than knowledge" but "brighter than ignorance."[48] Only entire beings, παντελῶς ὄντα, are entirely knowable and thus entirely true – if known they are always completely known as what they are.

The explication given so far, however, does not touch on what is very likely the most puzzling aspect of Socrates' conception, namely his explication of how beings and appearances are related to each other. What does it mean

[47] Cf. EDMUND HUSSERL, Logische Untersuchungen II.2, Husserliana XIX.2, ed. by Ursula Panzer, The Hague 1984, 589; EDMUND HUSSERL, Analysen zur passiven Synthesis. Aus Vorlesungs- und Forschungsmanuskripten 1918–1926, Husserliana XI, ed. by Margot Fleischer, The Hague 1966, 3. Cf. FIGAL, Unscheinbarkeit, also GÜNTER FIGAL, Gegenständlichkeit. Das Hermeneutische und die Philosophie, 2nd revised edition, Tübingen 2018.

[48] PLATO, The Republic 478c. Translation by Allan Bloom.

that something appearing is 'like' a corresponding idea? How can, for instance, something beautiful be 'like' the beautiful itself?

Socrates' answer to this question is briefly alluded to in the *Phaedo*, more precisely in his autobiographical retrospective. Here, Socrates explains the basic assumption of his philosophy, stating that it seemed to him necessary to flee into words (λόγοι) and to examine the truth of beings in what is said. And, as he adds, this would not be completely different from examining this truth in orientation to things (ἔργα), since things are not any less pictures than words.[49] Only the tenth book of the *Republic*, however, offers an extensive discussion of appearances as 'pictures' and thus makes an attempt to characterize appearances conceptually.

This attempt is led by the model of artistic representation (μίμησις). For example, what a painter painting a picture of a couch would achieve would not be a real couch, but only something that is 'like' a real couch – the shape of a couch realized in color on a two-dimensional board or canvas recognizable as a 'couch'. Instead, it is only an appearance (φαινόμενον) – appearing as something without being that as which it appears.[50] There is a form in the picture that appears as a couch, but is not a couch at all, just as portraits may be 'like' the portrayed persons without actually being them. Since the meaning of a picture understood in this way is the depicted, one has to know the depicted 'in reality' in order to understand the picture. One must also know what depiction is,

---

49 Plato, Phaedo 99e–100a.

50 Plato, The Republic 596c. The term "couch" for the Greek word κλινή is adopted from Allan Bloom.

namely the appearance of something that as appearance is different from being and, in this difference, dependent on it. Taking the two presuppositions together, one will recognize a depicted couch in light of this knowledge.

In the case of artistic representation, it makes sense to say that something pictured is 'like' the object depicted. What is to be seen in the picture, indeed, looks like the depicted object but is nevertheless different from it. This difference can even be made explicit with a picture, as it is the case with René Magritte's painting *La trahison des images*, 'the treachery of images', which shows a depicted smoking pipe and, below, also in oil paint, the writing *Ceci n'est pas une pipe* – this is not a smoking pipe. Also, the perspectival character of such a painted appearance is obvious. As a result of artistic representation, the picture will always be determined by the particular painter's view and technical skill. This perspectival view, however, can be compared with the depicted object and on the basis of such a comparison, can also be assessed. The picture can be more or less 'like' the object depicted, and in this regard, it can be examined and criticized. Taking the depicted object as a measure, one could discover what painters have omitted or represented falsely. Their depiction may, for instance, not be according to the true proportions of the depicted object.[51]

And so it seems that for Plato's Socrates it is precisely this potential to compare an appearance with the appearing object that makes artistic representation philosophically attractive. As a model, artistic representation offers a metaphorical designation of how beings and appear-

[51] Cf. Plato, The Sophist 235d–236a.

ances are supposed to be related to each other, and it also determines this relation as a hierarchical one. The model suggests the priority of beings over appearances.

Artistic representation, however, is only a model and as such, though suggestive, is not convincing. The model does not clarify how something beautiful can be understood as an appearance of the 'beautiful itself'. 'The beautiful itself' is not a depicted object, and a beautiful appearance is normally supposed as actually being beautiful and not as a fictional representation of something else like the smoking pipe in Magritte's painting. Nevertheless, it would be premature to reject Socrates' conception before having examined how he further explains his attempt to understand the relation between appearances and beings along the lines of artistic representation. Socrates does so in the tenth book of the *Republic*, in a passage that deserves particular attention because his explanation is in keeping with an especially illuminating discussion of what up to now has remained quite vague, namely his understanding of 'ideas'.

At first glance, the relevant passage seems to be helpful since it makes clear that the 'likeness' of appearing things to a model should not be understood all too rigidly. Instead of comparing two objects like a real couch and a picture that depicts a couch, it suggests being content with something as a kind of measure according to which appearances can be evaluated. In the *Republic* this requirement is supposed to be fulfilled by explaining the status of appearances with the paradigm of utensils. As Socrates points out, utensils have their "virtue, beauty, and rightness" – ἀρετὴ καὶ κάλλος καὶ ορθότης – in use, χρεία. Use is the measure for the producer of utensils, and accordingly the user of something, the one who is "most experienced," ἐμπειρότατος, in respect to the product, is the binding authority for the producer. The user alone has knowledge (ἐπιστήμη) of the used thing, whereas the producer only has "right trust" (πίστις ὀρθή) about it. Accordingly, the producer must rely on the user's advice.[52]

With the paradigm of utensils, Socrates also attempts to make sure that the knowledge of users – and thus real knowledge – is knowledge of ideas, or, as one can briefly call it, eidetic knowledge. For instance, the knowledge of how to ride a bicycle is not limited to a single particular bicycle or to a few of them. Having knowledge as a cyclist, one is able to ride every bicycle, provided that a particular bicycle allows reasonable use. If this is not the case, a cyclist will say that this particular exemplar is not a good bicycle and probably criticize its maker. The cyclist is able to do this on the basis of experience with at least a few bicycles but mainly through knowing how to ride a bicycle and what kind of object is required for this activity. In any case, particular bicycles only are examples for the eidetic determination of a bicycle as being appropriate for cycling. As Socrates would say, particular bicycles are more or less 'virtuous', beautiful' and 'right' in representing their eidetic determination.

The argument set out is persuasive and also largely plausible. Intelligent use, indeed, is eidetic knowledge, if eidetic knowledge can be understood as knowledge of something that is not primarily a single particular object, but rather the determinateness of certain kinds of objects

---

52 Plato, The Republic 601d–602a. Translations by Allan Bloom.

that are all accessible or usable in basically the same way. It follows then that every particular object is essentially determined in a way accessible or usable with the knowledge of this determination.

Knowledge of use, 'knowing how' to use something,[53] also ensures that the known correlate is not just an abstraction – as if the general notion of 'the bicycle' were constituted in ruling out all particular properties of particular objects so that a more or less clear cognitive image of the object in question remained. The knowledge, for instance, to ride a bicycle is not abstract, and accordingly the correlate of this knowledge, a bicycle in its usability, cannot be just an abstraction. Rather, it must be something that is truly knowable.

So, as one may conclude, it really is plausible to understand the knowledge of use as eidetic and its correlates as 'ideas'. It is very likely that because of this plausibility, Husserl adopted the argument in *Ideas I* where he states that an object ("*Gegenstand*") recognized in its meaning ("*Sinn*") is grasped as an 'originary self' ("*originäres Selbst*"),[54] and that meaning, again, normally belongs to the context of 'practical interest'.[55] Heidegger likewise adopted the argument in *Being and Time*, understanding things in general as utensils (*Zeug*) and defining the be-

---

[53] Cf. Gilbert Ryle, The Concept of Mind, London/New York 1949; Michael Polanyi, The Tacit Dimension, New York 1966.

[54] Edmund Husserl, Ideen zu einer reinen Phänomenologie und phänomenologischen Philosophie. Erstes Buch. Allgemeine Einführung in die reine Phänomenologie, Husserliana III.1, ed. by Karl Schuhmann, The Hague 1976, 332.

[55] Edmund Husserl, Analysen zur passiven Synthesis, Husserliana XI, 23.

ing of utensils as 'meaning relevant for use' (*Bedeutsamkeit*).[56]

Husserl and Heidegger, however, both refrained from understanding the 'objective meaning' ("*gegenständlicher Sinn*")[57] or the 'meaning relevant for use' (*Bedeutsamkeit*) of something as an 'entire being' (παντελῶς ὄν) and of saying that particular objects 'resemble' this being. And they were right in doing so. The 'idea' of something being is not at all itself 'a being', but rather constitutes or determines something that has a particular meaning *in its being*. Though particular objects only partly conform to their respective 'idea' – for instance, if they are not optimally useful – they nevertheless do not 'represent' this idea, but rather are directly determined by it. Accordingly, it may be more adequate to speak of *eidetic determinations* instead of 'ideas', not least in order to avoid confusing the determinations of beings with beings. Eidetic determinations are not beings, nor are they entities different from appearing objects. Rather, they are only objectively accessible with such objects, for instance the eidetic determination of a bicycle with particular bicycles.

The conception of eidetic determinations as beings is no longer relevant in Plato's later dialogues. It is difficult to say whether this is due to Plato's philosophical development or to his strategy as an author of theoretical plays, in which different positions not to be identified with his own are presented. There is some evidence, however, that

---

56 Martin Heidegger, Sein und Zeit, Gesamtausgabe vol. 2, ed. by Friedrich-Wilhelm von Herrmann, Frankfurt am Main 1976, § 18, 111–119.

57 Edmund Husserl, Cartesianische Meditationen, Husserliana I, ed. by Stephan Strasser, The Hague 1963.

Plato maintained the conception of ideas as discussed in the *Republic.* Provided that the *Seventh Letter* is genuine and thus really a kind of philosophical testament, Plato never ceased understanding ideas as beings. In the *Seventh Letter* the correlate of knowledge is characterized in a way very similar to its characterization in the *Republic*, namely as 'that which truly is' (ὅ … ἀληθῶς ἐστιν ὄν).[58] If the letter is spurious, only its author and not Plato himself sticks to this conception of ideas and has very likely adopted it from the *Republic.* This assumption would make it easier to understand why Plato's later dialogues can differ remarkably from the conception as Socrates develops it in the *Republic.* If the *Seventh Letter* is genuine, understanding the later dialogues becomes difficult.

Since Plato remains backstage in the dialogues – and obviously intended to do so like every playwright – his personal philosophical development is less interesting than what happens onstage. This, however, is a clear development – from a position quite close to that of Parmenides to a critical discussion of his philosophy. Intended as an improvement of Parmenides' conception, the conception of ideas presented in the *Republic* is still dominated by the notion of being. This Parmenidean legacy is not least confirmed by attempts to overcome it. Plato's later dialogues, *Parmenides*, *Theaetetus*, *The Sophist* and *The Statesman*, and especially *Parmenides* and *The Sophist*, offer a critical discussion of Parmenides' philosophy; the protagonist of *The Sophist* and *The Statesman*, an anonymous 'Eleatic stranger' or 'Eleatic guest', is a former apprentice of Parmenides who learns how to disen-

---

58 Plato, Seventh Letter 342b.

gage from his master and transcend the master's position with a conception of ideas that owes much to Heraclitus and little, if anything, to Parmenides. This conception retains the understanding of ideas as true correlates of knowledge, but no longer identifies them with 'entire beings'. Being is no longer a character of ideas. Instead, in the *Sophist*, being-ness (οὐσία) is conceived as an eidetic determination and thus as a correlate of eidetic knowledge. It can be explained as the possibility of other eidetic determinations to connect with each other (δύναμις κοινονίας) and thus form a complex set of determinations that, in its unity, is a being.[59]

From a point of view characteristic for the late dialogues, not only the Parmenidean conception of being, but also its Socratic revision appears as problematic and, as a consequence, becomes a topic of critical discussion. This discussion takes place in the dialogue *Parmenides*, which, in its first part, is a discussion between Parmenides and the barely twenty-year-old Socrates. Parmenides is ironically presented as a keen-witted, but also tricky critic of Socrates' conception of ideas. The dialogue shows how the Eleatic philosopher demonstrates to young Socrates the problems of his conception, and he mainly does so by making clear that these problems originate in the assumption that ideas are 'beings'. One example of a problem discussed in the dialogue is that many particular things cannot share one idea because it would thus be disaggregated in the manifold of things. This, however, is only possible if ideas are conceived as beings.[60] In the

[59] Plato, The Sophist 252d.
[60] Plato, Parmenides 131a.

dialogue, Plato's Parmenides and Socrates also discuss the problematic nature of the assumption that particular things can be 'similar' to ideas, like pictures are 'similar' to things or depicted living beings. As Plato's Parmenides argues, similarity between an idea and a particular being requires a second idea that provides a relation between appearing things and ideas and thus determines in which respect they are supposed to be similar.[61] Only if particular things and ideas are both regarded as beings, are criteria for similarity required, just as the similarity of two individuals can only be explained with determinations like height, shape, color of hair, or eyes etc. Since the idea introduced as a criterion for similarity has the same character as the first idea, another idea is required that guarantees the relation between the first and the second idea – and so on infinitely. The message indicated by such aporia is that Socrates' conception is not sound.

However, since this conception is obviously problematic, the question seems unavoidable as to why Plato's Socrates – or Plato – could ever find it attractive. Why did Plato's Socrates – or Plato – adopt Parmenides' conception of being and revise it, developing the conception of ideas to be found in the *Republic* instead of elaborating such a conception as independently as the Eleatic Stranger does in *The Sophist*? In Plato's case, this could, again, be explained with his philosophical development – when he wrote the *Republic* he presumably or probably did not know what he knew when writing *The Sophist*. Such an explanation, however, is not only guesswork, but also neglects the philosophical attraction of Parmenides'

---

[61] PLATO, Parmenides 132d–133a.

discovery of 'being'. Parmenides, as a reminder, introduces the notion of being in contrast to the unreliable mixture of being and non-being characteristic for the opinions of the 'mortals'. Being guarantees true knowledge, and it is precisely this assumption that is confirmed by Socrates' – or Plato's – conception of ideas as elaborated in the *Republic*, especially by the identification of the entirely being (παντελῶς ὄν) with the entirely knowable (παντελῶς γνωστόν).

The notion of being Plato adopts from Parmenides is also indispensable for the conception of appearance developed in the *Republic*. Understanding appearances with the paradigm of artistic representation cannot do without relating them to being. Appearances as defined by Socrates or Plato are deceiving only for someone not taking them as representations. As such, however, they are representations of beings and thus intelligible only in relation to beings. Accordingly, someone oriented to appearances is not isolated from being and is completely entrapped in false assumptions like the 'mortals' in Parmenides' poem. Appearances allow experiences of being, though not direct experiences of being itself.

The Socratic or Platonic conception of appearance is, however, not only an improvement in comparison with Parmenides' understanding of mortal confusion, but also offers an alternative to an understanding of appearances that could be designated as 'radical phenomenalism'. According to this position, appearances are not to be understood as appearances of something that could also appear otherwise. Rather, they are mere appearances and as such the only thing accessible. Accordingly, a refutation of this position would assert that there truly are beings that can be distinguished from appearances and experienced as such. This, again, could lead to the assumption that as true beings, they are correlates of knowledge.

The considerations on the 'entirely knowable' and the 'entirely being' in the *Republic* can be understood as such an, albeit tacit, refutation of radical phenomenalism. An explicit discussion of radical phenomenalism is to be found in a dialogue written later than the *Republic*, namely in the *Theaetetus*. In this dialogue, the position of radical phenomenalism is ascribed to the sophist Protagoras. It is articulated in a sentence according to which human beings are 'the measure of all things, of things being that they are and of things not being that they are not'.[62] As Socrates suggests, this sentence indicates that being can be reduced to appearances that are completely dependent on the experiencing person: everything 'is' for me just as it appears to me, and everything is for you just as it appears to you.[63] Appearances understood in this way are merely subjective.

If Socrates interprets Protagoras' sentence correctly, and if the sentence thus interpreted is true, then there is no difference between appearing and being and, as a consequence, there is no being at all. Such a reduction of being to appearing, again, is tantamount to the elimination of truth. To speak of truth, conversely, only makes

---

[62] Plato, Theaetetus 152a: πάντων χρημάτων μέτρον ἄνθρωπον εἶναι, τῶν ὄντων ὡς ἔστι, τῶν δὲ μὴ ὄντων ὡς οὐκ ἔστιν.

[63] Plato, Theaetetus 152a: οἷα μὲν ἕκαστα ἐμοὶ φαίνεται, τοιαῦτα μὲν ἔστιν ἐμοί, οἷα δὲ σοί, τοιαῦτα δὲ αὖ σοί.

sense if not every opinion and statement is legitimate, because things are what they are and in their very being are grasped only by opinions and statements adequate to them. If something appears to someone as red, for instance, it is admittedly taken as red by this person, but it is not necessarily red. The person opining it as red could be wrong, perhaps because of poor light. What truly is, however, never is only 'for me' or 'for you'. It simply *is*.

What, however, does it mean that something 'is'? How is 'being' to be conceived if the idea of eidetic determinations as 'entire beings' can be refuted as first demonstrated in Plato's *Parmenides*? If there are no eidetic beings or existing ideas – and this does, *nota bene*, not mean that it is meaningless to speak of ideas or eidetic determinations at all – the only beings left are appearing beings experienced perspectively. But are they beings or merely defective combinations of being and non-being? How can something appearing be, and how can it be conceived in its being?

It is quite possibly such queries that motivated Aristotle to radically rethink the question of being. He rejects the position as developed in the *Republic* with harsh words: to say that the ideas are paradigms and that the other things participate in them, is to speak emptily and to use poetical metaphors.[64] Ideas, then, are only accessible with appearing things that are eidetically determined in their appearance. With this understanding of ideas, however, the conception of being as developed in the *Republic* remains the starting point for further investigation. Aristotle was seemingly not impressed by the conception of being as a

[64] ARISTOTLE, Metaphysics I.9, 991a 20–22.

possible connection of eidetic determinations offered in *The Sophist* and at least in one respect this could be comprehensible: this conception lacks a discussion of appearance and thus of how appearing beings should as such be conceived. Revising instead the 'classical' Platonic conception as it is developed in the *Republic*, Aristotle adopts this problem and thereby affirms the 'classical' conception as the binding ontological scheme.

Aristotle restates the problem of being programmatically by stating that it seems to be impossible that being-ness is separated from the thing the being-ness of which it is, and thus introducing the key term of his own ontological conception.[65] The Greek term translated here as 'being-ness' is οὐσία, a noun that goes back to the word οὖσα, which is the feminine form of the participle in the present tense of the verb εἶναι. So 'being-ness' is a correct, almost literal translation. Using this term, Aristotle already indicates his solution of the Platonic problem. Ideas, he wishes to demonstrate, are not beings, but rather the being-ness of something that appears as being with its basic eidetic determination. Such programmatic summary of Aristotle's conception of course needs explication, and even Aristotle himself had to travel a lengthy route of conceptual clarifications. In order to understand the problem of being better, it is worth following him in detail. Though the Aristotelian conception, like the Platonic conception, will turn out not to be without its

---

[65] ARISTOTLE, Metaphysics I.9, 991b 1–2. It should be noted in this context that the term 'ontology' was not coined by Aristotle or any other classical Greek philosopher, but rather by R. Göckel (Goclenius) in the early seventeenth century. Cf. RUDOLPH GOCLENIUS, Lexicon philosophicum, Frankfurt am Main 1613.

problematic aspects, it is decidedly more revealing for the question of being and thus provides a solid basis for further discussion.

V. Being-ness

In order to explain Aristotle's considerations on being, one should first clarify the meaning of being-ness. What is 'being-ness', and how can being-ness be distinguished from being? Aristotle introduces his answer to this question with a general remark on the meaning of being. As he says, being is stated in multiple ways – τὸ δὲ ὂν [...] λέγεται πολλαχῶς.[66] From the outset, this statement goes beyond the conception of Plato's Socrates for whom, as has been discussed, being is nothing but the entire and unimpaired accessibility of eidetic determinations. Aristotle illustrates the diversity of being in drawing an analogy to the term 'healthy'. Something can be healthy in that it *preserves* health, like healthy food or exercise, but also insofar as it *produces* health, like a cure and medical treatment; or something can be healthy in *indicating* health, say the 'healthy coloring' of a person's face, and also insofar as something is *receptive* of it, like a living being that, after illness, has become healthy again and thus 'received' health.[67] All these ways of using the expression 'healthy' are factually appropriate in their diversity. Also, they refer to something common so that they cannot be reduced to homonymy – as if they were one expression

---

[66] Aristotle, Metaphysics IV.2, 1003a 33.
[67] Aristotle, Metaphysics IV.2, 1003a 34–1003b 1.

with different meanings that are completely independent from each other.

Just as something can be healthy in different respects, something can 'be' in different ways. And just as all different meanings of the expression 'healthy' are related to the health of a living being, likewise the different meanings of 'being' are related to one meaning or, as Aristotle says, to 'one' in terms of 'one nature' or 'essence' – πρὸς ἓν καὶ μίαν τινὰ φύσιν.[68] The manifold of being and, accordingly, the manifold meanings of the corresponding expression have a center that rules all different kinds of being. It is the *principle* of being, or, as Aristotle would call it in his language, the ἀρχή of being. It is *being-ness* that is this principle of being.

What, however, does 'being-ness' mean? The English expression that, as already noted, is a literal translation of the Greek term, can be understood in analogy for instance to 'correctness'. Correctness could be explained as the habitual disposition that enables a person to behave correctly. Accordingly, being-ness must be what enables something being to be. Being-ness, then, could also be called the *essence* of being, and not just by chance, since the expression 'essence' means the same as 'being-ness'. The Latin noun *essentia* goes back to the participle *essens*, which is an intensification of *ens*, being. So the essence of being is the being-ness of being.

The sketched and still very formal meaning of being-ness may become more concrete with Aristotle's explication of οὐσία in analogy to health. Since the analogy explains a structure, namely the structure of a mul-

[68] Aristotle, Metaphysics IV.2, 1003a 33–34.

tiplicity ruled by one single element, it also indicates that being-ness is not to be understood as isolated, but as ruling a multitude in a specific way. Just as different aspects of health can be discerned and understood as such in respect to health, one can distinguish different ways of being that all are bound to being-ness. Only thereby they are interconnected and thus form a manifold whole, each aspect of which only with respect to being-ness can be called 'being'. Such are the things that happen to being (πάθη οὐσίας), the way to being-ness (ὁδὸς εἰς οὐσίαν), destructions of being-ness (φθοραί), privations (στερήσεις), properties (ποιότητες), and what produces being-ness (ποιητικά) or allows it to be generated (γεννητικά). Aristotle also mentions negations of possibilities of being-ness or of being-ness itself.[69]

Aristotle's main point should also be plausible without having discussed in detail the different modes of being he introduces: it is always *something* that has properties or is produced or destroyed, and as with production or destruction as such *is* only as production or destruction of something. What, however, is 'something', and how can it be determined?

A first and almost self-evident answer to this question might be that that which has properties and undergoes different states is a *thing* or a *living being*. With a term introduced by Strawson, such entities could be called "basic particulars" and be characterized as "three-dimensional objects with some endurance through time."[70] Aristotle, however, would not have been happy with that, and a

[69] ARISTOTLE, Metaphysics IV.2, 1003b 4–10.

[70] STRAWSON, Individuals, 39.

closer look reveals good reasons for agreeing with him. Though it may seem plausible to say that it is something particular, for instance a chair that has a certain color and still is the same chair if the color is changed, one will easily discover that the sameness of the chair is not so easy to determine. A 'three-dimensional object' like a chair is not really the same once given a new color. It is a different object, admittedly not a completely different one since its form is still the same and since it can still also be used as a chair. But the form of a chair could also be changed, for instance by attaching armrests, or the seating of the chair could have been treated in such a way that it would no longer be possible to seat oneself on it. So because the identity of a 'basic particular' as defined by Strawson is not independent from the particular's properties, form, and states, it cannot be the 'one' referred to whose properties and states are understood as being.

As a consequence of these considerations, one could assume that it is the 'objective meaning' of something as defined by both Husserl and Heidegger, or, in other words, it is its eidetic determination that constitutes its identity. Something like a chair, then, would be what it is because it can be used in a certain way characteristic for a chair, and accordingly it would cease to be what it is, if it no longer had this meaning – a chair that cannot be used as a chair is not a 'real chair' and thus not chair at all so that one very likely would choose another chair. Thereby, however, one would confirm that the possibility of use, the 'objective meaning' of something is not restricted to a particular object. Taken as a general determination that can be applied to several or even many particular objects, the objective meaning of something is not understood as being-ness, but rather as a meaning that can also be conceived in abstraction from particular objects. Though one would have to admit that an objective meaning by definition must be the meaning of something, one could understand it without taking into account its particular realization with a particular something. It could just be taken as meaning concretized by a different object – like a linguistic meaning that could be articulated by different words or a number that could be taken as a number without regard to particular objects, the quantity of which can be determined by it.

These considerations are completely in line with Aristotle's. As he wishes to show, it is neither a 'basic particular' nor a general determination in reference to which particular properties and states could be called 'being'. Neither is it a composition of both, but something different and unique. It is being-ness, which as such can neither be separated from a particular object like a general determination nor identified with such an object. But how, then, is being-ness to be conceived?

Aristotle gives an initial and preliminary answer to this question in the first chapter of the seventh book of the *Metaphysics*. Repeating his general statement concerning the multiplicity of being, Aristotle now explicates his notion of being-ness by determining it as 'what it is and this whatever there' – τὸ [...] τί ἐστι καὶ τόδε τι.[71] This expression is not only unusual when translated. The original Greek version also differs quite radically from ordinary language use. That said however, the expression is not enigmatic. It combines a question – 'what is it?' – with a

---

[71] ARISTOTLE, Metaphysics VII.1, 1028a 11–12.

demonstrative that is joined with an indefinite pronoun – 'this whatever there'. Both parts of the expression are joined by 'and' (καί) and indicated as a unity by the prepended article 'the' (τό). As it seems, though, this unity can only be explained in distinguishing its two different aspects. Since, on the other hand, these aspects are both indispensable for the unity, they complement each other by revealing the unity as an interplay of its two aspects. Accordingly, being-ness can further be explained by saying what the two complementing expressions mean and how their complementary character can be understood.

To begin with, the components of Aristotle's expression can be explained as empty variables that indicate how they could be filled. The question 'what is it?' requires an answer giving an appropriate determination, whereas the second expression indicates that this determination must be conceived as referring to something 'there', 'before me',[72] so that the reference has a deictic character mostly indicated by expressions like 'this'. Being-ness, then, is being 'this determinate' – something determinate that as such can be there before one's face. So being-ness is different from Plato's 'entire beings', which, as such, are imperceptible. Being-ness must be localized, and thus it must be something that is really 'there'.

Since the two aspects of being-ness complement each other, all answers to the question 'what is it?' that designate being-ness must go along with a deictic gesture indicated by an expression like 'this'. Not all deictic determinations do, however, indicate being-ness, but, according to Aristotle's distinction between being-ness and other

---

[72] Cf. LIDDELL/SCOTT, A Greek-English Lexicon, 1197.

kinds of being, only those functioning without further determination. A possible answer to the question 'what is it?' could, for instance, be 'a color', say the color 'red' and, more precisely, a certain shade of red, which could be referred to by an expression like 'this red'. For a property like a color, however, there must be something determinate that has a certain color, even if color is the main object of attention. One might be mainly interested in different colors or different shades of a particular color and not in the colored entity one has before one's face. In choosing a cover fabric for a chair, one may use different cushions that function as samples. Though in this case one would speak about different colors or shades of it, the correct answer to the 'what is it?' question as an indication of being-ness would be, for instance, 'a cushion' and not, for instance, 'a pinky shade of red'. Primarily, a cushion would be 'there' and with it only a certain shade of red which in its being is dependent on the being of the cushion. Distinguishing 'this particular red' from another shade of this color, one thus, strictly speaking, refers to 'this red cushion on the floor'. In speaking of 'this red' one would only lose sight of the being one refers to.

These explications will only be helpful for understanding the function of being-ness if one remembers that being-ness must not be confused with particulars like cushions. A particular object like a cushion is something being – something of a certain shape, texture, and color – and as such it is a unitary and materially realized ensemble of determinate aspects that is adequately characterized with Aristotle's term σύνολος or σύνολον.[73] Such

[73] Aristotle, Metaphysics VII.11, 1037a 29–30.

a 'composite' is a being and accordingly not being-ness, which is the principle of being. As a principle, however, being-ness must be both present and distinguishable in a particular being. Referring to a particular being, it must therefore be possible to identify its being-ness. How is it possible to make such identification?

Aristotle answers this question by further refining his explication of being-ness. The overall strategy of this refinement is to identify being-ness with the *basic determinateness* of something. Restating his distinctive characterization of being-ness, Aristotle designates this determinateness as independent from other determinations. All these must be assigned to something else,[74] whereas the determination of being-ness is ascribed 'as itself' (καθ' αὑτό)[75] and thus provides a basis for all other determinations. Aristotle indicates this basic character of being-ness with the expression ὑποκείμενον which is translated into Latin as *subjectum* and can be translated into English as 'that which lies beneath'. Being-ness lies beneath all other determinations.

This characterization can easily be explicated and thus confirmed as plausible. Whereas a sentence like 'this is a couch' offers complete information, a sentence like 'this is big' would immediately prompt the question '*what* is big?' unless an answer to this question had already been given. So, in referring to a basic determination one indeed refers to 'something', to an 'entity', and not only to a property or state that only could be as a property or state *of something*. This explication so far leaves the

---

[74] Aristotle, Metaphysics VII.3, 1028b 36–37.

[75] Aristotle, Metaphysics VII.1, 1028a 23.

main point open, however. It does not yet explain the basic determination's status as being-ness. A basic determination could be regarded as being-ness only if it did not just form something's determinateness, but thereby also constitute its very being. Then reference to the very being of something must conversely be reference to its basic determination. Examined more closely, an example like the one just given will confirm this. However, it will also show that the very being of something is not identical with a basic determination as such. Whereas a particular basic determinateness is designated correctly by answering the question 'what is it?', the very being of something only comes into play with a demonstrative like 'this', especially if the demonstrative is stressed – '*this* is a couch' – and goes along with a deictic gesture. Such a gesture would not point to 'something' that has the character of a couch, but rather just to 'a couch' and thus indicate that what is there primarily *is* a basic determination. Only in being there, however, is a basic determination not only a general concept ascribed to something, but the being-ness of a being. So referring to being-ness does indeed require the two aspects introduced by Aristotle, namely an answer to the 'what is it?' question as well as a deictic gesture. Only with the deictic gesture, however, can the answer to the 'what is it?' question refer to something as being-ness. Being-ness, to resume, is an eidetic determination one could identify without taking it as a being and thus reiterating Socrates' or Plato's mistake.

The interpretation of being-ness just given is confirmed by Aristotle's expression for basic determinateness, namely ὑποκείμενον. The expression not only designates the determinateness of something 'as itself' and thus as the basis for all other determinations dependent on it, but also the factual character of this determinateness as a correlate of deictic gestures and statements. The preposition ὑπό does not only mean 'beneath', but can also mean 'before' so that the verb ὑποκεῖσθαι can designate something as lying before someone's face.[76] What, however, 'lies there' is not just something, but being-ness.

It is very likely that Aristotle's assumption of being-ness as 'lying there' will not be taken as self-evident. How can being-ness be 'something' that can be pointed to at all? Rethinking the chosen example, one will soon understand that this is not possible without something being. Though an expression like 'couch' does not designate a particular character of something, but rather a particular determinate 'something' as itself a couch, such a 'something' one can point to also is what Strawson would call a 'basic particular'. Deictic gestures essentially refer to something that can be seen or otherwise perceived, though they do not necessarily refer to something in its perceptibility. Pointing, for example, to a book lying 'there' on the table, one may mean the object pointed to primarily as a book and not as something visible. Undoubtedly, however, the book's determinateness as a book is 'there' with a particular visible object, more precisely with the object the being-ness of which it is. How can it nonetheless be distinguished from this object?

[76] Cf. Ernst Tugendhat, TI KATA TINOΣ. Eine Untersuchung zu Struktur und Ursprung Aristotelischer Grundbegriffe, Freiburg/München 1958, 14.

Aristotle answers these questions with a summarizing though not concluding definition of being-ness. According to this definition, being-ness is 'the eidetic determination being within' – τὸ εἶδος τὸ ἐνόν – whereof together with the matter the composite whole is disclosed as being-ness – ἐξ οὗ καὶ τῆς ὕλης ἡ σύνολος λέγεται οὐσία.[77] With this expression, which, by the way, was very likely inspired by Plato's *Philebus*,[78] Aristotle indicates how to conceive the constitution of beings through their respective being-ness: being 'within' a particular, an εἶδος determines this particular as what it is. This is a real or factual determination; it is not added to a particular by someone cognizing it. Cognition can only confirm what really is there as 'this determinate particular'.

However, one should stress again that according to Aristotle, determinate particulars must not be confused with their basic determinations. If Aristotle were to regard a particular and its basic determination as identical, he could not designate the determination as being 'within' the particular. Being 'within' a determination 'makes' or 'lets' something be what it is and thus allows reference to it in its being-ness. Accordingly, recognizing something as what it is, one refers mainly to its basic determination instead of the particular with its many and more or less obvious properties. Recognizing something as a tree, one refers to the tree-ness of the tree, which is its being-ness as a tree. A tree can never lose this tree-ness without ceasing to be a tree. It may lose its leaves, some of its branches, or parts of its bark and nevertheless remain what it is.

---

[77] ARISTOTLE, Metaphysics VII.11, 1037a 29–30.
[78] PLATO, Philebus 16d.

Moreover, one should note that according to Aristotle's summarizing definition, an eidetic determination is being-ness only as 'being within'. Taken separately, it has a general character with unspecified applicability. Jestingly alluding to Socrates, Aristotle illustrates this difference between being-ness and separate eidetic determinations by the example of a snub nose. [79] Whereas regardless of noses, the form of a snub nose could be determined as a particular case of hollowness or concavity (κοιλότης) when constituting a snub nose this form should be called 'snubness' (σιμότης). Snubness is the concavity of a nose and as such a concretization of concavity only possible with noses. This, however, does not mean that concavity turns into snubness because of a particular nose. It rather constitutes a snub nose being 'within' a nose. Being 'within' something a basic eidetic determination is the being-ness of this 'something'. And, as Aristotle indicates, it is matter (ὕλη) that by a particular being-ness is made a being – just as the matter of a nose is made a snub-nose by snubness.

Aristotle's conception of being-ness as explained so far may have some plausibility. This may be mainly due to the distinction between a basic determination and other determinations dependent on the basic one, and also due to the observation that referring to something determinate one would normally identify it directly with its basic determination. Something determinate essentially *is* this determination that, because of this, can be conceived as the determinate being's being-ness. However, Aristotle's conception will probably not be clear in every respect.

---

[79] Aristotle, Metaphysics VII.11, 1027a 30–33.

Several crucial questions have not yet been answered. So it is that one may wonder what happens with an eidetic determination without specified applicability when it turns into being-ness. For this modification, the role of matter seems to be decisive, but so far it has not yet become clear what Aristotle's conception of 'matter' is. Also, one may intuitively agree that a particular tree, for instance, is recognized as such with its basic determination. But why should one speak of something like 'tree-ness' instead of simply saying that in recognizing a tree, one grasps a tree as a tree? What else should 'tree-ness' mean other than that a tree is a tree? And why, then, should one distinguish between trees and their tree-ness, asserting that the latter is 'within' trees? What does this 'being within' mean, provided that it has a meaning at all?

Aristotle gives answers to all these questions with his conception of *becoming* (γένεσις) as it is discussed in chapter seven of the seventh book of the *Metaphysics*. With becoming, not only the 'within' of eidetic determinations becomes clear, but also the very status of these determinations and, going along with this, the very status of matter.

As to the concept of matter, it may nevertheless be helpful to explain in advance the term Aristotle uses. Aristotle's term, ὕλη, literally means 'wood', more precisely 'timber' or 'construction timber'. Understanding matter in this way as 'material', Aristotle reveals his orientation to the paradigm of technical production, and he also indicates that he regards matter as something dependent on construction and, even more, on the result of construction. The trunk of a tree, for instance, is not 'matter', but is only so if deemed appropriate for constructing something, say, roof beams. Matter, to conclude, is essentially functional. It is conceived as material *for* something like a product. Accordingly, the question what in particular an appropriate material for something might be, can only be answered in reference to the character of the product. For instance, timber is an appropriate material for roof beams, or, to take up one of Aristotle's favorite examples, ore is an appropriate material for a statue.[80] Such examples indicate that the status of matter can only sufficiently be determined in considering the functional context it belongs to, namely the context of production which, on its part, is a particular kind of becoming.

Becoming as Aristotle conceives it cannot be understood without reference to eidetic determinations. This is remarkable because eidetic determinations are excluded from becoming. Aristotle, like Plato, assumes that eidetic determinations as such are unchangeable. With becoming, however, something happens to them. What happens to them *is* becoming. With becoming, a basic eidetic determination becomes being-ness so that becoming, with a phrase from Plato's *Philebus*, could be characterized as 'becoming to being-ness' (γένεσις εἰς οὐσίαν).[81] In contrast to Plato, however, Aristotle does not conceive becoming just as the determining formation of something indeterminate, but rather as a revelation of what basic eidetic determinations as such have always already been. With his conception of becoming Aristotle insofar corrects the contrasting of a general eidetic determination and being-ness as it is illustrated by the example of the

[80] ARISTOTLE, Metaphysics VII.3, 1029a 3–4.
[81] PLATO, Philebus 26d.

snub nose. Becoming is not initiated with a general eidetic determination like 'concavity', but rather with an eidetic determination that is a specific mode of being-ness. Accordingly, Aristotle describes becoming as a process from being-ness to being-ness – from being-ness as initial to being-ness as result.

Though Aristotle distinguishes two kinds of becoming, namely natural becoming – which could also be termed 'growing' – and technical production, he seeks to show that the structure just sketched applies to both of them. Both are a process of realizing and manifesting an eidetic determination that as a process has initially been enabled by this very determination. As Aristotle says summarizing his considerations on becoming with two examples, in a certain sense health – as the particular aim of medicine – originates from health, just like a house – as the particular aim of architecture – originates from a house. The origin is respectively health and the house without matter; and what is originated is respectively health and a house that has matter. As Aristotle adds, medicine and architecture as technical skills can be identified with the respective eidetic determination of health and a house, whereas the eidetic determination of health or a house materially realized are the being-ness of a person being healthy and of a house as a house. Aristotle stresses, however, that both modes of eidetic determinations, the materialized one and the one without matter, can be called 'being-ness'. As he adds, he calls being-ness without matter the 'being what it was' (τὸ τί ἦν εἶναι).[82]

[82] Aristotle, Metaphysics VII.7, 1032b 11–14.

Certainly, these considerations need rather extensive comment and explication. It may be best to begin by returning to their leading assumption, namely that technical skill (τέχνη) of whatever kind can be described as knowledge of eidetic determinations – or quite simply: as eidetic knowledge. In contrast to Plato, Aristotle does not reduce this kind of knowledge to the knowledge of use, but also conceives it as productive knowledge. So whereas Plato or Plato's Socrates characterizes productive knowledge only as 'correct trust', with Aristotle's conception, both knowledge of use and knowledge of production become intelligible as versions of 'knowing how'. Thus, Aristotle conversely makes clear how 'knowing how' in general can work as a paradigm for eidetic knowledge as the knowledge of being-ness. By doing so, he underlines that eidetic determinations are not mere abstractions, and though not particular entities, are true correlates of knowledge.

Aristotle's argument can be explained in detail alongside his examples that are both illustrative and also function as paradigms. In order to cure someone, a physician must know what health is, just as an architect planning to construct a house must know what a house is. In both cases, such knowledge is not restricted to a particular situation and thus to a particular being. Health is basically the same for every living being, and however different particular houses may be, what they nonetheless have in common is that they are houses. So both examples show that productive knowledge must be knowledge of eidetic determinations.

Aristotle explains this in more detail with respect to health. In the first book of the *Metaphysics* he points out the essential difference between the eidetic knowledge of a physician and empirical therapeutic knowledge. Though therapy based on experience can be successful in several or even many particular cases, it lacks insight into *why* its effort could be effective. Empirical therapy is nothing but a reaction to factual states of living bodies suffering the likes of fever or pain and led by the experience that particular remedies, such as cool poultices, have often been helpful in the past. Physicians, in contrast, are able to determine particular diseases because they have an idea of how the normal state of a living body is disordered by a particular disease. This, again, requires insight into the normal state and its order or, briefly, into health.[83]

At any rate, someone is only a true physician if such eidetic knowledge is in place prior to curing someone. If physicians were to just try different therapies and expect one of them to be successful, then they would be practicing on the basis of more or less developed empirical knowledge, and not technical skill. Eidetic knowledge thus outlined is determined by its particular eidetic content, and that means: by at least one and essentially one basic eidetic determination. With eidetic knowledge, this determination, to put it in Aristotle's words, is 'the eidetic determination in the soul' (τὸ εἶδος ἐν τῇ ψυχῇ).[84]

In becoming, in the case of technical production, an eidetic determination that has been 'in the soul' or, as one could also say, 'in mind', is realized and made manifest. In architecture, Aristotle's second paradigm for techni-

---

83 Aristotle, Metaphysics I.1, 980b 28–981b 12.
84 Aristotle, Metaphysics VII.7, 1032b 1.

cally achieved becoming, this happens, first, in the architect's projection of a particular house as it becomes manifest with drawings and construction plans and then, second, by the work of different craftspeople coordinated by the architect. What, according to Aristotle, is realized in this work is not primarily a building made of concrete, stones, bricks, steel, wood, glass, or whatever other appropriate material, but rather the eidetic determination of the house as the architect has had it 'in mind'. The eidetic determination in the architect's mind is *identical* with the one realized with appropriate material at a particular place. This determination is the being-ness of something particular, in the case of architecture, a building that is there in its being-ness. For the sake of its realization and manifestation, however, the building's being-ness must have been known in advance of actual construction.

This consideration is not unreasonable. After all, how should real health or a real house be established if the knowledge how to produce health or construct a house did not include the reality of the house, or, to use another word, its being? Accordingly, what the leading eidetic determination producers necessarily have in mind is the being-ness of the entity to be produced. So in technical production, being-ness has to appear twice: once in the producer's knowledge and then in the product of knowledge. Becoming as Aristotle conceives it is, as it were, an eidetic determination's journey from mind to physical reality. In becoming, these two appearances of an eidetic determination are simultaneously unfolded and kept together.

Aristotle refers to this togetherness with an enigmatic terminological expression already quoted, but not explained: τὸ τί ἦν εἶναι. This expression combines the infinitive 'to be' with the question 'what was it?' and conjoins them with a definite article. The whole expression can almost literally be translated as 'the *to be what it was*'. The question 'what was it?' indicates being-ness in knowledge as *what* a particular product *was* before its production, whereas the infinitive indicates the being there of the product that can be pointed to.[85] What *was* in mind is what the product factually *is*.

With this explanation, the specific function of Aristotle's terminological expression may become clear. The expression connects the status of an eidetic determination as something being known with its status as 'being within' and thus as being-ness as defined in the eleventh chapter of the *Metaphysics*. One should note, however, that this connection is not symmetrical. Defining the 'to be what it was' as 'being-ness without matter', Aristotle indicates that the expression refers to being-ness as a correlate of knowledge rather than to being-ness having become manifest with a product. Regarding a product in respect of what it *was*, one is, indeed, not primarily attentive to its factual being. Without this factual being, however, the eidetic determination in question could not be called 'being-ness' at all, but rather would just have a general character as Aristotle exemplifies it with concavity. However, for being attentive to what a being in its being-ness 'was', its factual and thus also material being is only a starting point.

---

85 Cf. Tugendhat, TI KATA TINOΣ, 18.

Such a marginalization of material being is not restricted to the attentiveness on being-ness as a correlate of knowledge. It is also characteristic of Aristotle's understanding of being-ness being manifest with a particular material being. Both aspects are revealing about Aristotle's understanding of 'matter' as such. In order to clarify this understanding, one should first stress that being as constituted by being-ness must not be confused with the factual presence of particular objects the components of which can be distinguished and described. The being of being-ness is not a composition of eidetic determinations, one of them basic and the other of material as it is, for instance, used in the construction of a house. Rather, Aristotle regards the being of a particular house as solely enabled by being-ness, more precisely by the eidetic determination 'house' that becomes manifest in matter and thus is 'within' the particular house. By identifying something particular as a house, one implicitly refers to this eidetic determination that makes a particular being be a house. Such dominance of eidetic determinations may become especially clear with production insofar as it shows how eidetic determinations *precede* particular objects or, as Aristotle calls them, composite wholes. Something produced 'was' necessarily what it essentially is – otherwise it could not have been produced. If the basic eidetic determination of something is thus leading the process of production, it is unlikely to lose this dominance in the product. Architects lead by the basic eidetic determination of a house while planning and constructing a house will, in the case of success, make manifest just the determination they were led by. Though eidetic determinations could not be understood as being-ness without their being materially manifest, matter is only the medium of manifestation and not inherent to the manifestation of being-ness as such.

The question of how this manifestation can be conceived leads to the center of Aristotle's conception of being-ness. Aristotle's answer to these questions is indicated by a single term the importance of which is proved by the fact that Aristotle invented it – because it seems he could not find an adequate expression in ordinary language for what he wished to designate. The term is ἐνέργεια, mostly translated into English as 'actuality'. While this translation is not wrong, it does miss an aspect that is decisive for the specific meaning of Aristotle's expression. This aspect can be clarified by explaining how the word is generated.

The root of the word is ἔργον, which generally designates the product of whatever production and, in this sense, means 'work'. The first part of Aristotle's word, ἐν, is a preposition that means 'in', whereas its last part, -εια, is a suffix that, like '-ness' or '-ity' in English, is used in Ancient Greek for generating nouns. So Aristotle's word means something like 'in-work-ness'. What he wishes to designate with his expression is an activity that is not completed by the product that is its result, but rather is complete *as* activity – an activity that, as it were, actually *is* its product. Thinking or viewing, for instance, are not practices devoted to the production of something, but rather are activities complete without an external result. Aristotle, however, does not restrict his term to designating a specific type of activity. The term also or even mainly applies to every reality that is not the reality of a product, but rather reality in process. Such a reality can justly be called 'actuality', albeit in a broad sense that goes beyond the literal meaning of the word, which originally has its roots in *actus*, 'action'.

Aristotle explains his understanding of ἐνέργεια in the eighth book of the *Metaphysics*. His explanation is led again by the paradigm of technical production and especially by the example of constructing a house. With this example, Aristotle wishes to clarify the difference between the house understood as a being in its being-ness, and the house just as a composed whole of formed material. According to this distinction, the question of what a house is can be answered in two different ways. One could say that a house consists of stones, bricks, and wood, but, as Aristotle says, in doing so one would determine a house only in its potentiality (δυνάμει) since all components mentioned are matter. However, calling a house a receptacle that can shelter living beings ('bodies') and utensils one would designate its actuality.[86]

A few sentences later, Aristotle summarizes his consideration with a quite uncommon yet illuminating example, namely the calmness of the sea (γαλήνη). In the case of a calm sea its water is matter whereas the actuality and form (ἡ ἐνέργεια καὶ ἡ μορφή) is the evenness (ὁμαλότης) of the sea.[87] According to this explanation such a smooth sea is not to be conceived as 'water with a certain property, namely evenness'. Rather it is the evenness that makes the sea how it actually is. Evenness is the actuality of the sea if the sea is so smooth that one could not even think of a storm with raging waves. Even-

---

[86] ARISTOTLE, Metaphysics VIII.2, 1043a 14–18.
[87] ARISTOTLE, Metaphysics VIII.2, 1043a 24–26.

ness, to reiterate, is not just a property of the sea's water, but rather its actuality: the water is nothing other than a potential that can be determined by an actuality like evenness.

Aristotle's former example of the house should also be understood in this way. It may even be more significant in that it makes the determining character of actuality more intelligible. A house that is not a receptacle for living beings and things is not a house at all. It may be a building made of bricks and even look like a house, but by being uninhabitable, like the brick sculptures designed by Per Kirkeby, it will not be a house.[88] It is *habitability* that makes a house a house so that the material building, understood as a constructed whole is a house only as long as it is habitable. If it were seriously run-down or damaged one would simply call it 'a former house'.

Conceiving a house's being-ness as its meaning is also plausible in respect of its design and production. What an architect has in mind while drawing and elaborating construction plans is something habitable, a building in its 'objective meaning' as Husserl would say. Only if this meaning is realized by design and production is a house made into that which its future inhabitants would understand as a house. So production and use – provided that, at the moment, inhabiting a house can be called 'use' in a very broad sense – are two different kinds of knowledge that have basically the same correlate, albeit one that is present in two different ways for architects and inhabitants. Thus, the objective meaning of the house, its eidetic

[88] Cf. GÜNTER FIGAL, Erscheinungsdinge. Ästhetik als Phänomenologie, Tübingen 2010.

determination, is twofold. As the eidetic determination an architect has in mind, it determines both activity as well as the product. On the other hand, it determines the inhabitants of the built house insofar as they inhabit it. Both these sides of an eidetic determination are like two sides of the same coin, or as Aristotle would possibly prefer to say, as the two aspects of the 'being what it was'. As Aristotle states, the 'being what it was' is there as eidetic determination and also as actuality – τὸ γὰρ τί ἦν εἶναι τῷ εἴδει καὶ τῇ ἐνεργείᾳ ὑπάρχει.[89] It is being-ness without the actual experience of something, the being-ness of which it is as well as the determinateness of a being and also of its experience.

Recalling a definition of the 'being what it was' previously given, one might find this characterization puzzling. Explaining production before, Aristotle determined the 'being what it was' as 'being-ness without matter',[90] which could be regarded as incompatible with saying that the 'being what it was' can be there 'in actuality'. This objection, however, is not to the point, if actuality and matter are not the same, something Aristotle makes abundantly clear. Realized in matter, an eidetic determination is not explicitly understood as being-ness, but rather in reference to the respective being as a composed whole (σύνολον). Regarded as being-ness of such a being, however, an eidetic determination is there in actuality. Experiencing this actuality, one is less attentive to the material object before one and more so to the 'objective meaning' as manifest with a being. This 'objective meaning', then,

[89] Aristotle, Metaphysics VIII.3, 1043b 1–2.
[90] Aristotle, Metaphysics VII.7, 1032b 14.

dominates this being, whereas its materiality only allows the meaning to be objective and dominant in its actuality.

If these considerations are appropriate, Aristotle's key definition of being-ness, namely the definition of being-ness as 'the eidetic determination being within' (τὸ εἶδος τὸ ἐνόν)[91] must not be understood as referring to an eidetic determination's reality as something provided by matter. Rather, it refers to an eidetic determination's actuality that as such is the reason why the composed whole can also be understood as being-ness. By calling the composed whole 'being-ness', one takes it in its determinateness that, strictly speaking, is the actuality of its determination. Actuality is the original character of eidetic determinations as being-ness. In their actuality, such determinations form the intelligible reality of something that, in its intelligibility, has to be strictly distinguished from its material existence. According to Aristotle, matter does not even enable reality, but is nothing more than a necessary condition for being-ness as actuality to take place. As to this, Aristotle's conception of matter comes very close to the conception of the indeterminate place and space (χώρα) as developed in Plato's *Timaeus*.[92] Admittedly, Aristotle's conception of matter cannot be reduced to this. As already pointed out, his very expression translated as 'matter' or 'material', ὕλη, is closely associated with technical production and coined in orientation to one of his favorite examples, namely the construction of houses. In any case, however, matter only allows the eidetic determination's actuality to be there, whereas this

---

[91] Aristotle, Metaphysics VII.11, 1037a 29.

[92] Cf. Figal, Unscheinbarkeit.

being there is as such an integral aspect of an eidetic determination's actuality.

Applying this result to Aristotle's preliminary definition of being-ness as 'what it is and this whatever there' (τί ἐστι καὶ τόδε τι), one can demonstrate the consistency of his conception. As actuality *of an eidetic determination*, being-ness is determinate (τί ἐστι), and is thus an answer to the question 'what is it'. As *actuality* of an eidetic determination, however, a particular being-ness is 'this determinateness there' (τόδε τι). Being there, it is what Aristotle calls ὑποκείμενον: it is accessible as a 'substance' for other kinds of being like properties, states, incidents, and alterations that are dependent on it. As such a 'substance', it is also a 'subject matter' for recognition and knowledge. The character of this substantiality is actuality. As Aristotle says, actuality means that the particular subject matter is there – ἔστι δὴ ἐνέργεια τὸ ὑπάρχειν τὸ πρᾶγμα.[93] So actuality fulfills both characters of being-ness introduced by Aristotle at the very beginning of his pertinent investigation. Understood as actuality, being-ness is *objective determinateness*, or, equally, *determinate objectivity*.

In order to understand Aristotle's conception adequately, it is all-important not to forget that the determinateness of this objectivity as well as the objectivity of this determinateness is *eidetic*. Aristotle's conception of being-ness is mainly about eidetic determinations and thus not as different from the Platonic conception as one might assume, considering how sharp a line Aristotle draws between his own and his master's conception.

---

[93] Aristotle, Metaphysics IX.6, 1048a 30–31.

Nonetheless, Aristotle's conception is much more consistent and convincing mainly, if not exclusively, because of the concept of actuality. Being in actuality, eidetic determinations are objective and nevertheless not beings. As being-ness, they are to be experienced with beings, but they must not be reduced to them. Rather, with being-ness beings, 'composed wholes', can be understood as *being* what they are. On account of being-ness as actuality, they exist in in their actual intelligibility.

This correspondence between actuality and intelligibility deserves some closer attention. Though Aristotle clearly overcomes the problems that make the Platonic conception developed in the *Republic* so problematic, he nonetheless affirms the Platonic understanding of being as being intelligible and thus would, in principle, also agree with Plato's assertion that something entirely intelligible, παντελῶς γνωστόν, must be entirely being, παντελῶς ὄν. He would add, however, that the entirety in question is not that of a being, ὄν, but rather that of an actual being, εἶναι, and more precisely of being-ness. It is actuality that entirely is, which is so because in actuality there is nothing that is not actual – nothing that is not yet actual or not actual any longer. There is nothing unrealized in actuality as there is in an activity like production or growing. Such an activity, Aristotle calls it κίνησις, is essentially incomplete, since as long as it lasts its goal is not yet attained. Actuality is also entirely being, because it does not originate in and emerge from possibility. It has always entirely been what it is.

Aristotle illustrates this characteristic of actuality with seeing and thinking. One never begins to see or to think, but in seeing one already has been seeing, and in thinking one already has been thinking.[94] With seeing and thinking then, an antecedent state of not having been seeing and thinking must be unimaginable. In any case, by realizing the eidetic determination of a house, architects have already understood what guides their work. Whenever this determination is realized in concrete, stones, bricks, steel, and glass and thus allows understanding the produced entity as 'house', it has already been present in an architect's mind – in the 'soul' as Aristotle says. In its actuality, an eidetic determination is always entirely what it is – without matter as well as materialized. It is always entirely being and, according to the Platonic assumption, therefore entirely knowable.

Being entirely knowable, actual eidetic determinations are entirely true. They are true as such, and thus the experience of their truth is not dependent on particular situations as it is the case with everything that undergoes change. The assertion that 'this house is uninhabited' can be true in one situation and false in another, for example. As Aristotle explains, the assertion is 'composite' – to be uninhabited does not essentially belong to a house, as does its habitability. Rather, its being uninhabited is 'added' to what a house essentially is, whereas one cannot understand something as a house without understanding that it is habitable. A house can be instantly understood in its habitability – intuitively, or, as Aristotle says, it can only be 'touched' and 'said' in its actual eidetic determination.[95] Saying that a house is habitable is not an assertion because it is not 'composed' like the sentence

---

94 Aristotle, Metaphysics IX.6, 1048b 23–26.
95 Aristotle, Metaphysics IX.10, 1051b 24.

that 'this house is uninhabited'. It is a simple designation of something unitary that adequately designates what is there just as what it is. Adopting a term from Husserl, one could call such a statement 'adequately evident'.[96] However, it can only be evident because the stated actuality is evident. This actuality is simply and immediately there as what it is.

This should in one respect be plausible – understanding a building as a house one understands it intuitively as a building that is habitable, and habitability could thus justly be called a house's eidetic determination. It may, however, be doubted that the correlate of such an understanding is 'actual' in Aristotle's sense. This doubt is not brought up arbitrarily, as if Aristotle would not give reason to it. Instead, Aristotle's favorite example of the house supports critical arguments against his conception. One can quite easily demonstrate that the habitability as the eidetic determination of houses is not something 'actual' but rather, as the very expression indicates, a *potential*. This can be explicated in at least two respects.

Firstly, a house is habitable even if no one is living in it. It is habitable regardless of actual inhabitants, and must be so because otherwise potential or actual inhabitants could not experience habitability. Habitability enables habitation and thus precedes it. Though it is confirmed in habitation, it is nonetheless not dependent on it. Houses – such as those of fine artists or writers that have been turned into museums – could be habitable without being inhabited ever again.

---

[96] Cf. EDMUND HUSSERL, Erste Philosophie (1923/1924). Zweiter Teil. Theorie der phänomenologischen Reduktion, Husserliana VIII, ed. by Rudolf Boehm, The Hague 1959, 26–35.

Speaking of habitability, one will, secondly, have an idea of what is meant, and this ideal can be explicated: a house deemed habitable should, for instance, be stable at the very least and should provide shelter from heat, cold, rain, wind, and storm. But it will not be easy to generally determine in detail what habitability means. The expectations and requirements of different potential and actual inhabitants are most likely to differ. Nonetheless, one and the same house can satisfy such varying expectations and requirements, although this is only possible if its potential of habitability is not determinate in every respect. Rather, it must include indeterminacy in order to allow different realizations of the potential's determination.

The partially inherent indeterminacy essential to a determination like habitability will also be relevant for architectural design and construction. Even if architects extensively discuss their design and construction plans with respective builder-owners and seek to achieve a bespoke house, the result of their work will never be exclusively appropriate for a single way of habitation. Despite all previous determinations, the result of architectural achievements may even be surprising for the clients so that they may discover a more or less fresh way of habitation with a new house. Such a dwelling may also be discovered in alternative ways by its new inhabitants and thus reveal previously unknown aspects of its habitability. Likewise in this respect, the eidetic determination of a house as it leads architectural work and is understood in habitation will be the determination of a potential and as such include aspects of indeterminacy.

One could object to these considerations by arguing that a single example does not provide solid ground for revising a whole conception like Aristotle's conception of being-ness. A second and no less significant example, however, may show that understanding being-ness as potentiality is not bound to a particular exceptional example, but is rather a consequence of Aristotle's investigations. This example is the human being.

According to Aristotle, the being-ness of human beings is made explicit by a linguistic determination of soul (ὁ τῆς ψυχῆς λόγος).[97] Though this is only a lapidary remark, it is not difficult to grasp what kind of determination Aristotle has in mind. He very likely does not think of just a simple definition (ὁρισμός) that combines a general determination with specific differences,[98] of such a kind that human beings could be defined as 'rational living beings'. What Aristotle says about definition in the *Topics* – and what has become a sort of canonical definition of definition – is only a formal characterization, and examples like the one given – 'rational living being' – are not meant to be complete and sufficiently detailed. On the other hand, however, definitions as Aristotle understands them are far from being 'definitive'. What is instead required, is not a conclusive formula, but rather a sufficiently concrete conceptual description, for which, in the case of human beings, a detailed investigation of life in general and human life in detail would be a necessary condition.

Aristotle has developed the main aspects essential for such an investigation in his treatise *On the Soul* (*de an-*

---

[97] Aristotle, Metaphysics VII.11, 1037a 28–29.

[98] Aristotle, Topics, 103b 15–16: ὁ ὁρισμὸς ἐκ γένους καὶ διαφορῶν ἐστιν. Quotations are taken from: Aristotelis Topica et Sophistici elenchi, ed. by W. D. Ross, Oxford 1958.

ima, περὶ ψυχῆς). In order to do this on solid conceptual grounds, he firstly introduces a formal characterization of what he understands as 'soul'. This formal characterization is of special interest for understanding the very status of being-ness. As Aristotle points out, the soul is being-ness as the eidetic determination of a body that has the potential of living.[99] This, again, is explained by a term that, like ἐνέργεια, is specific for Aristotle's conception. The term explains the status of an eidetic determination as being-ness, and it does so in an especially illuminative manner.

According to the explanation Aristotle gives of his preliminary characterization, the soul is 'the first completion of a natural body that has the potential of living' – ἐντελέχεια ἡ πρώτη σώματος φυσικοῦ δυνάμει ζωὴν ἔχοντος.[100] The term just translated as 'completion', ἐντελέχεια, originates from the adjective ἐντελής, which means 'complete', more precisely the completeness of an action that has reached its aim. What is ἐντελής is no longer 'in the making' and thus not still possible, but actual. In this far, ἐντελέχεια is synonymous with ἐνέργεια.

Against this background, Aristotle's distinction between 'completion' and 'first completion' is especially interesting. A 'first completion' is not mere possibility that can be realized and is recognizable as possibility only after it has been realized.[101] On the other hand, however, a first completion is also not actuality either, but prior to actuality and thus, as it were, something between poten-

---

[99] Aristotle, On the Soul, 412a 19–21. Quotations are taken from: Aristotelis De anima, ed. by W. D. Ross, Oxford 1956.

[100] Aristotle, On the Soul, 412a 27–29.

[101] Aristotle, Metaphysics IX.3, 1047a 24–25.

tiality and actuality. As already indicated with the translation of Aristotle's definition, it is a potential, but a *complete potential* – i.e., one that in order to be complete does not need to be transformed into reality, but is as a potential of what it is supposed to be. Only because of its completeness can a potential be understood as being-ness.

This characterization of a 'first completion' can be concretized with Aristotle's basic considerations on the soul. As being-ness of a 'natural body', the soul determines what and how such a 'natural body' *is* – *nota bene* not its material qualities and properties, but its being alive. As Aristotle shows, living beings are what they are in having certain faculties that are more or less specific to them. These faculties – in *On the Soul* Aristotle discusses digestion and reproduction, perception, and rationality – are not necessarily always actualized. A living being not actually perceiving something remains, for instance, what it is: a living being capable of perceiving. Its being-ness is not constituted by its actual perceiving, but rather by its faculty to perceive, namely by perception.

Perception could be called a 'property', although one should add that it is a *disposition* and therefore a special kind of property.[102] Dispositions are, firstly *permanent* properties and as such different from properties living beings – or things – only have occasionally. Animals, for instance, may be hungry or thirsty, but they will not constantly and essentially be so. In contrast, they have the faculty of digestion, and they would not lose this faculty if they did not eat anything for a certain time. A pane of

[102] Cf. RYLE, The Concept of Mind; FIGAL, Unscheinbarkeit.

glass has the disposition to be fragile, whereas it can be temporarily clean or dirty.

The constant character of dispositional properties is relevant for how they are related to someone or something. Secondly, dispositions are not properties a living being or a thing '*has*', but rather how someone or something '*is*' – the life of living beings with visual faculty is essentially determined by this disposition, and accordingly a living being that loses this faculty is specifically challenged and will have to live other than before. On the same strength, fragility is essential for a pane of glass that, without being fragile, would otherwise not be a pane of glass at all.

So dispositions are permanent properties essential for the being of someone or something. However, as such they are, thirdly, to be distinguished from properties that are *permanently manifest*. Such a property is, for instance, the color of fur an animal like a cat has. Perception, in contrast, may be concealed, even to a living being itself. While a sleeping living being will not or barely perceive something, it nevertheless retains its perception. And as to a pane of glass, a material quality like hardness that is permanently manifest is different from fragility that only becomes manifest if the pane breaks.

Though dispositions are factual properties essential for the being of someone or something and independent from manifestation, one would, admittedly, not attribute the likes of perception to a living being if this living being had never before been experienced as perceiving. Ascribing perception to an animal or fragility to a pane of glass must be evidenced by direct or indirect reports on viewing animals or breaking glass. Nevertheless, a disposition like visual sense is *not fulfilled* by actual seeing just as the process of producing is fulfilled by the accomplished work. A particular actuality of a disposition instead *confirms* it, and other actualities of the same kind would do so repeatedly. Such particular actualities will more or less clearly differ from each other to reveal only how a disposition *can be* actual and never realize the disposition as such. No actuality exhausts a disposition, whereas the process of producing a particular work is exhausted as soon as this work is accomplished. Hence for dispositions, activities actualizing them are secondary. Such activities are dependent on their respective disposition, only to be understood in *tracing them back* to a disposition, whereas production in process is dependent on the possible reality of a product and thus cannot be understood without *anticipating* such a product.

The character of dispositions as explained also determines an ensemble of dispositions like the one Aristotle conceives as 'the soul'. Accordingly, one may conclude that the soul as such is not actual, but rather a potential that can never be actualized completely and utterly. Nevertheless, Aristotle understands it as the being-ness of a living being. Just like the being-ness of houses and in general of products 'usable' in whatever way, this being-ness is also a potential. If the conception of being-ness applies only to living beings and products like houses or tools, one can conclude that *being-ness as such is potentiality.*

The ontological importance of this result cannot be overestimated. Revealing the inherent problems of Aristotle's ontological conception, it leads to a critical discussion of how the question of being-ness can be pursued in terms of Aristotle's conception without reiterating its problems. In order to initiate such a discussion, it may be helpful first to give a more detailed account of Aristotle's ontological problem. On the one hand, Aristotle does everything to revise the Parmenidean-Platonic conception of being. He does so without doubting its basic assumption of an entirely being that is entirely knowable, but in order to find out how to maintain this assumption without aporetic consequences. However, this solution, and first and foremost the conception of being-ness as actuality, is incompatible with Aristotle's own descriptions of being-ness in particular, since these descriptions reveal being-ness as potentiality and, in particular, as a determinate potential. Being-ness as potentiality cannot be conceived in terms of the Platonic idea of 'entirely being', and accordingly it cannot be entirely knowable or known. Thus it cannot be 'true being' and not even like 'true being' in Platonic terms, namely being without any inclusions of negativity. Rather, a potential includes indeterminacy, and necessarily so because otherwise it could not be actually confirmed in different ways. This kind of indeterminacy, however, is not to be confused with the indeterminacy of appearances explained by Plato's Socrates in the *Republic*. It is not 'the dark side' of something that is withheld from recognition, but rather an *indeterminacy that is a character of its specific determinacy*. It is mainly because of this that indeterminacy being-ness is then the kind of determinacy it is.

As can be illustrated by Aristotle's paradigmatic examples, such a revised conception allows a much more appropriate description of being-ness in relation to beings. The eidetic determination of a house that enables an architect to design and construct houses – the 'house in the soul', the house without matter which generates the materialized house, as Aristotle puts it – cannot be some kind of mental picture of a particularly accomplished house. In this case, an architect would have no choice but to design and construct the exact same, perhaps only slightly varying house over and over. The leading eidetic determination would then be akin to an anticipated copy of the architect's product. Normally, however, architects do have a choice, and this can only be so if the eidetic determination leading an architect's work is a potential. Because of this, architects are able to consider alternatives and decide in favor of particular solutions. Moreover, good or excellent architects will design buildings individually, adjusting them to particular purposes and specific surroundings. So their buildings, even if identifiable at first glance as manifestations of a certain architect's style, will not be the result of boring repetition, but original works of art. And as such, they will offer new and original insights into the potential of a house.

The eidetic determinateness of living beings basically has the same character, meaning it can be described quite similarly. Dispositions like perception and rationality, for instance, do not determine a living being completely, but rather allow many, if not infinite, actualizations. Perception and rational consideration will and even should be different in different situations and in reference to different objects, otherwise it would hardly be possible to do justice to the experienced situations, persons, and things. So in order to be successful, the behavior of living beings cannot be rigidly predestinated by their dispositions, and, as a matter of fact, is not predestinated in this way. This is especially evidenced by intelligent living beings, human or not, that can often be surprising. While their behavior could not be expected, it will, on the other hand, always be within the scope of their respective ensemble of dispositions.

As these examples show, the specific indeterminacy of eidetic determinations does not exclude understanding a particular basic eidetic determination as the being-ness of particular beings. In principle, Aristotle's determination of a living being's 'soul' as its being-ness is convincing and so is his description of architecture as set out by the being-ness of a house. Being-ness conceived as potential, however, cannot be conceived just in the Aristotelian way – as though it were sufficient to replace actuality by potentiality and leave the conceptual setting as before. Rather, conceiving being-ness as potentiality will change the whole setting. Because of its indeterminacy, it cannot be the objective meaning of something or someone that dominates its experience as being in the way Aristotle evokes with his conception of 'actuality'. Being-ness will instead be less dominant, possibly even inconspicuous. It will more be like a frame than an 'actual' over-all determination of something, and going along with this, the particular being will draw more attention rather than being just like a place at which being-ness takes place. It will not disappear behind its being-ness, but rather be experienceable as a particular or even individual instance of its being-ness.

This assumption can be explained by further discussing the foregoing examples. A particular house must surely be identified as what it is, and this will necessarily be achieved on the basis of its 'objective meaning'. Moreover, this objective meaning is surely not an abstraction, but the objective determinateness of something. Inhabiting a house is an authentic experience of its being-ness, and in order to be experienced this way, something like a house must really have a determinate objective meaning. Experiencing a particular house in its being cannot, however, just be reduced to the experience of its objective meaning, its 'habitability'. This meaning covers and allows a broad range of possible particular manifestations of houses. What it means to inhabit a house then will not only be dependent on the house's objective meaning, but also, and not to a small degree, on the particular house's character. Experiencing a house as a particular architectural work, one will always also be attentive to its particularity as this becomes explicit, not least in comparison with other particular architectural solutions.

A particular house as correlate of experience, to recap, will not only be like a materially provided place for the actuality of the respective eidetic determination. Rather, it will be a house in its – not at least material – particularity and individuality. Especially if it is a work of art, it cannot be reduced to an objective meaning of whatever kind. Architectural masterpieces like Frank Lloyd Wright's *Fallingwater*, Ludwig Mies van der Rohe's *Villa Tugendhat*, Alvar Aalto's *Villa Mairea* or Tadao Ando's *Benesse House* are not just houses fulfilling certain purposes, but singular places that allow unique aesthetic experience. Not only artworks of this kind, however, provide individual experience as described. Many houses are individuals or at least particulars in different respects. Living in a wooden house is different from inhabiting a house with brick or concrete walls. Old houses stand out from contemporary ones, smaller ones from big, spacy ones. Though all these different houses have the objective meaning of a house, each is something of its own, being there as it is – being in a way that as such cannot be reduced to its being-ness because without this being-ness it could not be what it is.

The same applies to a large extent to things – utensils, pieces of furniture, or books – and certainly even more to living beings, especially people. As individuals, people cannot be sufficiently and appropriately understood as an ensemble of their respective dispositions, but lead their lives as individuals and thus often surprisingly so. As already mentioned, people do not normally just adhere to predetermining patterns of behavior, but rather act in response to the singular requirements of situations. Activities are essentially determined by the reality they refer to and are embedded in. Accordingly, they cannot be sufficiently explained by reducing them to the dispositions they are enabled by.

As a consequence of these considerations, the relation of being-ness and being is to be conceived in a way that differs considerably from Aristotle's conception. Whereas Aristotle lets beings be almost absorbed by their being-ness, in reducing 'matter' to 'material' determined by the form it is used for and also to an indeterminate place for the manifestation of being-ness in its actuality, a conception that is attentive to the particularity or even individuality of beings will regard being and being-ness as *different*. Accordingly, one main task of such a conception will be to offer a more precise and detailed characterization of this difference.

Stressing the difference between being and being-ness, an allusion to Heidegger's 'ontological difference' as exposed in his 1927 lectures on 'the basic problems of phenomenology' can hardly be avoided. However, the difference Heidegger introduces is that of Being ('*Sein*') and being ('*Seiendes*'),[103] and 'Being' as Heidegger understands it is 'Being as such', and not the being-ness of something particular conceived as the particular's eidetic determination. Thus understood, the difference of being-ness might bring Plato rather than Heidegger to mind. Admittedly, the ideas Plato's Socrates discusses in the *Republic* are not being-nesses, but assumed to be beings. Like being-nesses, however, they determine everything that 'partakes' of them, being essentially different from what it partakes of. Everything partaking of an idea is not an entire being, but an appearance. Accordingly, one might assume beings determined by their respective being-ness to be appearances.

The Platonic conception of appearance, however, could not really be helpful for understanding the difference of being-ness and being. As has been shown, this conception includes the determination of appearances as 'resembling' beings and as representing them. Beings, however, cannot be appearances of that kind. They do not 'resemble' their respective being-ness, and they do not represent them like pictures represent something depicted. On the other hand, neither can beings be appearances in terms of radical phenomenalism – simply because they are beings and as such cannot be reduced to subjective conception or construction. So one should

---

[103] MARTIN HEIDEGGER, Grundprobleme der Phänomenologie, Gesamtausgabe vol. 24, ed. by Friedrich-Wilhelm von Herrmann, Frankfurt am Main 1975, 454.

follow neither the Socratic-Platonic nor the radical phenomenalistic way, but seek a different conception of appearance instead. To this end, a more extensive discussion of appearance is needed.

VI. Appearance

Despite its inherent problems, the Socratic-Platonic conception of appearance should not be left completely aside. Socrates' remarks on the perspectival character of appearances do at least grasp something essential, since nothing can be an appearance without being experienced from different points of view. This perspectival character of appearances, however, cannot convincingly be explained in contrast to being. Though it is indisputable that something of a certain weight may seem light to one person and heavy to another, this difference cannot be completely reduced to the respective condition of these two individuals, thus rendering the weight's appearance as something merely subjective. Rather, it is in keeping with something of a certain weight that can be experienced differently, just as with a poetical or philosophical text that can be read and interpreted in different ways. And just as a text does not allow every reading and interpretation, neither will something of a certain weight allow every experience. Under normal conditions of experience, for instance, a feather could never be described as 'heavy', and in the same way a poem on joy hardly can be read as expressing sadness.

These considerations allow the meaning of 'appearance' to be determined more precisely. Something appearing is not just there *for someone* in such a way that its appearance is completely dependent on the experiencing person's perceptive and cognitive disposition. Rather, something appearing is there as itself in a particular possibility of itself and thus cannot be contrasted to being. Appearing belongs to the being of something that as such can be there in different ways. Appearances, then, are the objective manifestations of something that can neither be reduced to one of its manifestations, nor grasped without them. When experienced, something of a certain weight will always appear as more or less heavy and never as just something of a certain weight. Whatever the case, it will be weight that someone lifting or carrying a particular object would experience. Though often experienced in different ways, weight is an objective quality.

The objectivity of weight, however, is not something those experiencing it would especially care about, and because of this, weight is an especially suitable example for Socrates' intention to demonstrate that appearing has to be distinguished from being. The appearance of lightness or heaviness is primarily relevant for those experiencing something and only to a lesser extent for the experienced object as such. So someone may find a suitcase heavy and, expressing this, probably mean that carrying the suitcase is an uncomfortable or even arduous task. Another person may provide help by offering to carry the suitcase and assuring that it appears less or not at all as heavy to them. It is, however, improbable that both will compare their respective experiences of the suitcase in order to find out more about the suitcase's weight, and thus the different appearances of the weight remain unconnected. Though both experience the suitcase as an object having weight, they are primarily concerned with what the weight of the suitcase means for each of them and their particular activities. Accordingly, they would not reflect that both of them, having different capacities for carrying loads, do not understand the appearing weight as an effect of their respective subjectivity, but as weight. Their respective capacities are only different conditions under which something like a suitcase having a particular weight would appear. Their respective experiences are not regarded as contributing to exploring the appearing object in its quality of weight.

It would be another matter with beings that as such are objectively experienced with their appearances. The objectivity of such objects could be called 'strong' whereas in contrast the objectivity of a quality like weight would be 'weak'. Whereas weak objectivity has a tendency to be absorbed by the subjective, or to say it with a term coined by Husserl, the 'noetic' side of its appearing,[104] strong objectivity emerges with a manifold of connected appearances. Not by chance is something experienced, for instance, as 'heavy' not primarily regarded as an object, but only under the aspect of an object's property. As Aristotle has shown, properties are not independent objects, but dependent on particular objects. However, the dependency of a property can also be understood in relation to those doing the experiencing, which is tantamount to a marginalization of its objectivity.

How, in contrast, different appearances can be connected in order to investigate something in its objectivity should be immediately evident in view of something that in shape and surface quality cannot be grasped at a

[104] Cf. HUSSERL, Ideen I, Husserliana III.1, 202–205; FIGAL, Unscheinbarkeit, 115–120; FIGAL, Gegenständlichkeit, 131–153; 166.

glance. All multi-dimensional objects are such because they have different sides that do not appear simultaneously. This also applies to a sheet of paper, the back of which cannot be viewed together with its front, and even more evidently to three-dimensional objects. Looking at the front of such an object, one will miss its back, and, accordingly, only several looks at the object back and forth will reveal what it is. This applies all the more so to objects one cannot be hand-held because they are too big or too heavy to be moved. In such a case, one has to walk around an object and take in different points of view to grasp its various appearances.

Since the objects described are multi-dimensional, their being cannot be separated from their appearances. Rather, the object *is* only in different and combined appearances that, belonging to the object, are not primarily dependent on those experiencing them. An individual will have to take up various particular vantage points to experience the object adequately. An object's set of different appearances presupposes how experience of the object is possible. Thus, appearance is not constituted in experience, but is prior to it.

Considering the experience of appearing objects more closely, one will soon realize that it is not only presupposed by the experienced object. To take different particular views of an object, and thus of its set of appearances, is a *spatial* experience, meaning that the object's set of appearances must as such be spatial. Appearances like the ones described are determined spatially, for instance by particular places that function as points of view, by distances one has to keep from something in order to experience a particular aspect of it, or by ways one has to take in order to experience appearances in a particular order. So as a set of appearances, an object is determined spatially. Multi-dimensional objects are never without their spatial conditions of appearance and accessibility.

Spatial conditions also apply to appearances that are not to be experienced from vantage points, from particular distances, or on ways leading around them. Likewise, the appearance of weight is spatially determined – lifting something of a certain weight or carrying it over a certain distance is a spatial experience. This spatiality, however, remains mostly implicit because it is not primarily experienced as that of an object, but rather as enabling the activities performed by individuals. So the spatiality of an appearance like weight is, as it were, hidden in the experiencing person's spatiality as that of a person's potential of activities.

In contrast, the spatiality of appearances becomes especially obvious with beings that are not objects in a strict sense. Too big to be objects, they allow something objects would not normally allow, namely to sojourn inside them. This becomes clear with buildings since their appearance is not only spatially determined, but rather an appearance of space. With buildings, appearance and space as the enabling of appearance are intertwined in such a way that the spatial character of appearance becomes obvious.

This needs some explanation. A building can be viewed from afar or at close range, and architects will often take this into account when designing not just an isolated building itself, but its surroundings plus the ways leading to it as well. Such ways then are integral parts of a building,[105] allowing its outside structure to appear differently from varying distances, while placing the building's appearance in the context of its surroundings. Inside a building, however, the intertwinement of space and appearance is even more evident. The routes to be found within a building are provided by the building itself, so that viewing a room inside a building, one also views particular options of its experience. This, again, confirms that appearances cannot be separated – albeit distinguished – from their enabling, which is also the enabling of their accessibility.

A building also demonstrates that appearing beings cannot be experienced without their respective set of appearances. Simple once-and-for-all access to a building is impossible. A building is never 'just there', although canonical views, often captured in photographs, may suggest this. A building in appearance is the unitary multitude of its different appearances.

If it is thus possible to make the appearance of buildings become especially clear, the foregoing considerations should lead to a general and sufficiently differentiated understanding of appearance. To this effect, one should first note again that no appearance is singular, but rather belongs to a plurality – or at least a duality – of necessarily different appearances. Something only appears if it can appear differently. Otherwise one would not speak of the appearance of something, but rather say that it simply is what it is. The plurality and diversity of appearances is, secondly, spatially enabled. Something often appears

[105] Günter Figal, Ando. Raum, Architektur, Moderne, Freiburg 2017.

differently from different points of view because its difference is spatially determined – as different locations or distances, inside or outside. Thirdly, these points of view must not be confused with the views of individuals. Rather, people must adopt a particular point of view in order to experience something as appearing in a particular way. So to repeat the main gist of these considerations, appearances are not something primarily 'subjective', but are different possibilities of something to be there, or, as one can also say, *to show itself*. Something appearing can also show an experiencing person how it appears under particular spatial conditions. These are not primarily the conditions of appearing to someone who has taken up a particular point of view but, beyond this, the conditions of appearing as such.

It may be possible to understand this better by considering that the expression 'to appear' often has a largely *emphatic* meaning. Someone appearing can draw attention by coming to the fore – much like an actor appearing on stage. This emphasis of appearing is already dominant in the meaning of the corresponding Greek expression: φαίνεσθαι originally means 'to come to light'.[106] Appearance, in this regard, is nothing merely normal. Appearances are accentuated in contrast to what can preliminarily be called 'non-appearance'. Only in contrast can appearances draw attention.

The contrast between appearance and non-appearance is not necessarily like that of an actor who suddenly enters a previously empty stage so that this comes as something of a surprise. Everything, experienced in whatever

---

106 Liddell/Scott, A Greek-English Lexicon, 1912.

way, appears, and only little of what appears is surprising. However, nothing can appear without a certain contrast. In order to appear, everything must be foregrounded in some way.

Unlike these event-like appearances, but also in contrast to something non-appearing, are, for instance, the different sides of a building that are experienced by walking around it. Regarding the building, one becomes aware of the appearance of a particular side in contrast to the sides in 'adumbrations' ('*Abschattungen*'), as Husserl would say. Even more important, however, is a kind of contrast that can be illustrated by the difference between fore- and background, as in a painting featuring the portrayed figure of a person. Like the figure in a painting, everything appearing is silhouetted against a background that is less distinctive and thus recedes. Such a backdrop is not invisible. In not being absent, an appearance can be present in contrast to it. It is there, but, unlike an appearance, is *inconspicuous*. It is the inconspicuous that enables appearing.

Inconspicuousness can also be illustrated with the foregoing examples. A building experienced by walking around and through it will appear only partially. One will only have a view of one side of it or of parts of a room – no interior can be viewed in its entirety because one has to be inside a room in order to view it, and, in viewing one corner, one would lose sight of the walls behind. These walls, however, are not concealed or otherwise beyond the range of experience. One would at least sense the walls behind, knowing intuitively that, being in a room, one is surrounded by walls. Without the walls behind, the room would not be a room, and likewise a building viewed from the front would not be a building without a back. With the viewed front of a building the unviewed sites are there, inconspicuously, enabling the front to appear.

An actor's appearance also needs the inconspicuous, more precisely the inconspicuousness of the stage, at best a dark stage that, together with a spotlight, allows the actor to draw the audience's attention. However, though all eyes are directed to the actor, the stage, dark as it is, is not simply ignored. Rather, it is viewed together with the actor, not intentionally, but rather as the setting in which the appearance of the actor is made possible.

These examples clearly show that the inconspicuous, enabling something to appear, has spatial character. The dark stage and the dark backdrop of a portrait are places that 'receive' the actor or the portrayed figure, and, withdrawing from attention, they are free spaces that allow the actor and the figure to reveal themselves. The aspects of a building not actually viewed make the one viewed appear as belonging to a three-dimensional entity like a building. They make the building appear in its whole breadth.

The characters of space mentioned – place, free space, and breadth – would of course need further explication in order to become sufficiently clear.[107] Discussing the appearance, however, in order to clarify the appearance character of beings, one will regard another question, also concerning space, as more pertinent. As has been shown and as can be confirmed by the examples of an actor on stage and of a building, an appearing being is a set of appearances. An actor on stage will normally perform different activities, and a building appears in diverse aspects

---

[107] Figal, Unscheinbarkeit.

that are to be experienced from various perspectives. Though the actor's actions and the building's facades and aspects are a manifold of appearances, one will normally not doubt that they are the appearances of one single actor or building. They belong together in a characteristic way and can be distinguished from other appearances surrounding them. This *unity of appearance* in a set of appearances allows understanding what appears as a 'being'.

The unity of an appearing being is different with different beings. So the manifold actions of an actor are unitary when performed by the same person. It is the animated bodily appearance of the actor that unites his different actions – all these are performed as modifications of this appearance proving its animation. In the case of a building, the unity of its appearance will be, viewed from outside, its self-contained form and, viewed from inside, the continuity of its rooms.

None of these unities can be neatly separated from the manifold of appearances with which a living person or a building, and likewise a thing, are experienced. The unity that makes a set of appearances a being, is not central to which particular appearances are attached, as clothes are to a person. Rather, such a unity is like a boundary that includes a certain set of appearances and excludes all others. Taking up a term used prominently by Husserl, one could also call such a unity a *horizon*; more specifically, the 'inner horizon' ('*Innenhorizont*') that something itself is, in contrast to the 'outer horizon' ('*Außenhorizont*') of its surroundings.[108] Conceived as 'inner horizon', a be-

[108] EDMUND HUSSERL, Erfahrung und Urteil. Untersuchungen zur Genealogie der Logik (1938), ed. by Ludwig Landgrebe, 7th edition, Hamburg 1999, 28–29.

ing is not separated from its appearances. It is instead the unitary set of appearances that it actually is and can be. Experiencing something, then, means to experience appearances belonging to a particular horizon, which includes a set of factual and possible appearances and thus defines a particular being.

So far, particular beings have only been considered as how they immediately appear. This immediacy, however, is not necessarily experienced along with concrete understanding. For instance, one could view a building without knowing what kind of building it is, and things may be unknown except in that they are things. In Paul Valéry's Platonic dialogue *Eupalinos*, Socrates speaks about such an 'ambiguous object'.[109] Though experienced as spatial beings, things like this object or buildings that are just recognized as 'structures made of bricks' are not known in their being-ness, or, to take up an explanation of 'being-ness' given before, in their 'objective meaning'.

It has already been discussed how being-ness as objective meaning is to be conceived. The understanding of buildings and things like tools could be designated as a kind of 'knowing how' that is confirmed by an adequate use of something so that no explicit definition of the being-ness in question is required. If slightly modified, this explanation of understanding a particular being-ness can be generalized and thus also be applied to the being-ness of living beings. Also, to understand a living being as what it is does not require an explicit definition. It is suffi-

[109] Paul Valéry, Eupalinos ou l'architecte, in: Œuvres, ed. by Jean Hytier, vol. 2, Paris 1960, 79–147; Figal, Unscheinbarkeit, 102–106.

cient to know how, for instance, an animal would behave and, correspondingly, how to adjust one's own behavior to that of the respective living being. Other human beings are likewise understood in this way. Understanding persons means to take their expressions and actions as manifestations of a personal life that correspond to those of one's own life in essential reciprocity as well as to know how, through one's own expressions and actions, to 'respond' to those of the other person. Conceived in this way, knowing how proves to be not only technical and practical, but also communicative.

An understanding of being-ness as sketched can become reflective, and, as a consequence of reflection, a particular being-ness could be more or less extensively described and made explicit. In reference to an individual, this would mean a determination of which expressions and activities are characteristic for someone as a person, and accordingly, the being-ness of a particular thing could likewise be grasped by determining what one could do with such a thing. In both cases, one would not simply describe how persons in particular live and how things are used, but rather understand factual activities and factual use as manifestations of particular human faculties or of objective dispositional properties respectively. Such an understanding would refer both to the being-ness of someone or something as the potential of a being and to an appearing being. But how is such double reference possible? How can an appearing being be understood and described in its being-ness, and how will an understanding of a particular being-ness reveal a particular being? How is the difference between being-ness and being concretely grasped in understanding?

One can answer these questions by first investigating more closely the understanding of a thing in its meaning, say a utensil like a pen. Viewing such a utensil lying on a desk, one does not necessarily grasp its purpose immediately. This would surely be so if one had learned how to use a pen, and if such 'knowing how' has been acquired as an eidetic knowledge, it can be applied to every pen, provided that a pen functions as something to write with.

This functioning, however, cannot be reduced to a writer's competence. Rather, it is an objective character of the pen, and not just one among others. It makes a pen a pen and not only to look like one, and can therefore be called the pen's being-ness. This being-ness is not identical with the object lying there on the desk, but neither is it added to it – as if the object's function was identical with its use and thus only ascribed to it. The object really *is* functional as such, and nevertheless its function is not plainly to be seen.

On the other hand, however, the pen's function is not concealed – as if the pen were an 'ambiguous object' in terms of Valéry's Socrates. Viewing the pen's materialized form, one will discover how precisely elements have been put together, and accordingly one will very likely assume that it is functional in whatever way. By understanding the pen's purpose and testing what could be done with it, one may possibly find out that the pen's tip, if applied to paper, leaves traces, and so one will have almost discovered the function of the pen. Though not obvious, the pen's function appears indirectly, at least to a certain degree, with the pen. Conversely, the pen does not appear as such without its function. As a structured product, the pen does not appear without at least an indication of its function; and with its proper function it appears as a pen.

This description can be taken as paradigmatic for the interrelation of being and being-ness, and this interrelation would accordingly be that between an appearance or a set of appearances and a particular meaning that enables the appearing being to be what it is. This meaning will only appear indirectly with the appearance – it cannot be directly viewed. Nevertheless, it determines appearance as enabling something to appear as *what it is*, for instance of a pen as a pen. Being-ness, so far explained, is enabling. It enables a specific mode of appearance.

In order to conceive the relation between being-ness and being more concretely, the example of a pen and its being-ness, namely its function, may again be helpful. This function is not as easy to grasp at first glance as it may seem, since one might hesitate to identify it purely with writing. One could also draw with a pen, underline passages in a book, or scribble while making phone calls. So the function of a pen includes different activities that only have something quite unspecific in common, namely drawing lines, which is more an indication of what one can do with a pen than a sufficient designation. This somewhat unspecific function of a pen is grasped by intuitive understanding of a field of activities that cannot be exhausted by detailed description, since it may include activities not yet taken into account. In any case, it will exclude innumerous others. Thus, the intuition expressed in a phrase like 'something for drawing lines' does not refer to a manifold of particular activities more or less clearly imagined, but rather to a kind of boundary line – to a horizon. It is a horizon including the possibilities of something, some of which are known while others are unknown – a horizon that is a boundary line for the inclusion and exclusion of possibilities and as such a determinate and correlate of intuitive knowledge. Accordingly, one could call this horizon 'eidetic'. It is nothing factual that would have to be described in its complexity, but rather something simple and as such, according to Aristotle, something only to be 'touched' and 'designated'.[110] Being-ness, then, is the eidetic horizon of a being that lets this being be what it is.

This conception of being-ness can also be illustrated with Aristotle's paradigmatic examples for being-ness, namely the house and the soul, and thus possibly be explained more concretely. Understanding the being-ness of a house as 'habitability', one will immediately know what that means, but nevertheless find it difficult to explain in detail the possibilities of habitation provided by a house. Habitability is a possibility that can be realized in different ways, some of them possibly familiar, others vaguely known, and most of them not imaginable. It is for this reason that habitability cannot be exhaustively determined. Taken in its being-ness, a particular house will be an appearance defined by an intuitively graspable eidetic horizon of possibilities. Its actual state, including its structure, proportions, size, and position will indirectly offer the possibilities defined by this horizon to experience. The possibility of habitation will not appear, but only indirectly with the particular house. Thus, how-

---

110 Aristotle, Metaphysics IX.10, 1051b 24.

ever, as the house's eidetic horizon, it will allow the particular house's meaningful appearance.

Since a house's being-ness is inexhaustible by particular experience, a house appearing in its eidetic horizon will not be reducible to particular subjective ways of inhabiting it. A house and likewise any object that can be understood in the same way, is not determined as "something in order to" ('*etwas, um zu*') as Heidegger characterizes things discoverable in the world.[111] The routine use of things for a particular purpose in everyday life may lead to the conviction that particular objects only have this purpose. Realizing, however, that specific purposes belong to an eidetic horizon that lets things essentially be a potential, will lead to another view. One will understand that things the being-ness of which is an eidetic horizon including a more or less broad range of possibilities must be objects in and of themselves. Only as basically independent from being used in a specific way can they 'offer' possibilities to users. So the only alternative to the reduction of things to specific purposes is not to conceive them as "mere things" ('*bloße Dinge*') as Heidegger suggests.[112] Rather, things can be useful in particular ways and nevertheless remain as objects just standing there as defined by their horizon. Though not being things that can be experienced just as objects, houses too 'stand there' in a way comparable to things. Despite the objective character houses in one respect have, they are

---

[111] HEIDEGGER, Sein und Zeit, GA 2, 92; English translation is quoted from: MARTIN HEIDEGGER, Being and Time, trans. by Joan Stambaugh, New York 1996, 68.

[112] HEIDEGGER, Sein und Zeit, GA 2, 92; HEIDEGGER, Being and Time, 68.

not objects, but built space and as such cannot be experienced from the outside alone. However, through offering habitation their offering character becomes even more obvious.

Understanding being-ness in this way also allows the being-ness of living beings to be conceived without the assumption of an ontological gap between inanimate and animate beings, but also without drawing problematic analogies. Aristotle introduces such analogies, conceiving living beings in orientation to the paradigm of technical production and, as a consequence of this, speaking of an animal's flesh and bones as of 'matter' – as if an animated being would have been formed in appropriate material. Like things and buildings, living beings too – plants, animals, and humans – stand by themselves as what they are. Being in such a way, they are defined by the horizon of their possibilities which can be intuitively grasped as their animation or, as Aristotle would say, their 'soul'. In contrast to the possibilities of things, those of living beings are primarily not for someone else, but rather *their own*. They are faculties to live that become manifest, for instance, as growing, nourishing on something, perceiving, moving, or, in case of humans, as thinking, deciding, and performing actions. As Aristotle has shown with his conception of the soul as a 'first completion', these appearing activities do not realize, but rather confirm the faculties they are founded in. As a set of faculties, the 'soul' of a living being does not need to be realized and thereby completed since it is already complete. As such a completion, however, it is a potential and thus can only be grasped intuitively as a non-appearing horizon of possible appearances. All these appearances, again, are modifications of the being that a living being is, namely of its living body. They are bodily appearances, centered on a living body that as such is what it is as enabled by the being-ness of its 'soul'. The 'soul' never appears directly, but rather allows the appearance of a living being that, being animated, modifies its appearance again and again and, being as a being its potentiality, nevertheless remains what it is, irreducible to any particular appearance.

To conclude these considerations, one should first note that the suggested revision of Aristotle's conception of being-ness is basically affirmative. Instead of reducing the ontological question to one singular being, namely '*Dasein*', as Heidegger does, the revision argues for keeping up the assumption that *every* being as such is grounded in its being-ness. But neither are Aristotle's formal characterizations of being-ness to be rejected. They are at least partly compatible with the suggested inversion according to which being-ness is not actuality, but, following Aristotle's examples, potentiality. Indeed, the specific potential of something or someone as defined by its eidetic horizon makes something or someone be what it, and respectively, she or he *is*, and it follows that a determination of this horizon answers the Aristotelian question 'What is it?' (τί ἐστι). However, since the horizontal definition of something necessarily includes indeterminacy, by referring to something or someone, one would not indicate an actuality that is 'something there' (τόδε). What is there, instead, is a particular being, the being-there of which is accentuated by the indeterminacy belonging to its eidetic horizon. It is 'there' defined by its eidetic horizon and thus irreducible to its actual appearance. Since the being-ness of a particular being is such a potential, it cannot function as an underlying ground (ὑποκείμενον). Rather, it has the character of a horizontally defined, inexhaustible depth, and it is this depth that, as its being-ness, is 'within' every particular being and in contrast with its appearing surface.

As already noted, this contrast or difference between being-ness and being is essential for the suggested revision of the Aristotelian conception. As the horizontally defined potential of something, being-ness cannot constitute the being of something dominating it through the actual presence of a basic eidetic determination. Only particular beings can be 'present', and they are so as appearances. Eidetic horizons, including determinate and indeterminate aspects of potentiality, do not as such 'appear'. They only appear with particular beings, enabling them to appear repeatedly and differently as what they are.

As a consequence of these considerations, a twofold understanding of the appearance of beings becomes necessary. On the one hand, what is called 'being' would be the objective content of genuine appearances. Though not every being necessarily appears, every appearance – in contrast to a mere semblance or pretense – must be an appearance of something being. Otherwise an appearance could not be understood as something showing itself, but only as deception or as subjective appearance without objective content.

Something being that appears does not necessarily appear as a determinate being. It may lack a distinct form like a cloud or a heap of sand, or it may be like the ambiguous object Valéry's Socrates speaks about. Though having a more or less distinct shape, an ambiguous object is not eidetically determined as what it is, and according to Aristotle, it could therefore not be regarded as a unitary being.[113] However, as Aristotle, presumably involuntarily, concedes, such an eidetic determination is not the necessary condition for being. He implicitly concedes that a heap of sand also 'is' – and even more so an ambiguous object that is confirmed by its appearance as a distinct object. So eidetic determinations cannot constitute being. They, so to speak, only *augment* being in such a way that something eidetically determined would be something of a different and more distinct kind of being. If clouds, heaps of sand too, and, even more so, ambiguous objects are beings, then this more distinct kind of being is dependent on a kind of being that, with Husserl's term, can be called 'primordial'. Primordial beings are there with each more or less distinct appearance.

The distinction between eidetically determined and primordial being is of decisive importance for a philosophical investigation of being in general. Being, then, is not an exclusive theme of an 'ontological' inquiry in the Aristotelian – and thereby also Parmenidean and Platonic – tradition. Rather, with a phenomenological investigation of appearance as a self-revealing of something or someone, being is more or less explicitly thematic. And if being-ness is bound to beings as confirmed in appearance, the investigation of being-ness, Aristotelian or revisionary, is dependent on the phenomenological clarification of primordial being. With a philosophical reflection of this dependence, ontology as an investigation of being-ness would become an integral part of phenome-

---

113 Aristotle, Metaphysics VII.16, 1040b 5–10.

nology. Phenomenology is not restricted to an investigation of primordial appearances, but can also devote itself to clarifying the appearance of beings augmented by being-ness and thus take up the topics of traditional ontology.

This is an ontological approach within phenomenology that differs from Husserl's reduction of ontological questions to 'purely logical basic concepts' ('*rein logische Grundbegriffe*'),[114] and also from Heidegger's identification of phenomenology with ontology on the basis of the ontology of human '*Dasein*'. It is an approach that allows phenomenologically discussing the question of traditional ontology and thus of metaphysics, namely the question of being as motivated by the question of truth.

What is required in response to this question is a reminder of a formal characterization of being and truth as well as a clarification of how truth is available. A phenomenological answer to this, however, will not lead to a conception of philosophy as privileged ultimate knowledge, but rather show how philosophy can be devoted to truth and likewise reflect on the boundaries and blank spaces of knowledge. In order to show this, one has once more to discuss the question of truth, this time, however, not only formally, but rather by taking up the foregoing ontological discussion and, according to the difference between being-ness and being, seeking to clarify how a truth of being-ness can be distinguished from a truth of being. Provided that these truths belong together, the discussion of truth will prove to be about twofold truth.

---

114 HUSSERL, Ideen I, Husserliana III.1, 27.

VII. Twofold Truth

Truth, to remind of this, could be characterized as the correlation between something that really is – and is true in this sense – and a conviction justified by believing or knowing what really is and thus being true. Such a conviction can be articulated in an assertion that is true, stating what really is. This correlation is asymmetrical because the truth of convictions and assertations is dependent on the truth of being. Convictions and assertions can only confirm what 'truly' is. By this confirmation, often expressed with an emphatic use of the term 'is', one indicates that one is truly interested in the factual state of being.

In connection with the foregoing discussion on being and being-ness, however, this characterization needs some specification. According to a distinction introduced by Aristotle and already mentioned,[115] the being-ness of something is 'touched' and linguistically expressed immediately, whereas a particular being in its particularity can only be referred to in composite statements. The habitability of a house is something unitary, whereas a house in its particularity is something complex. It has different properties and undergoes different states that can be attributed to it as to a house that, being a house, simply is what it is. Accordingly – and in accord with Aristotle – one has to distinguish complex or composite

[115] Aristotle, Metaphysics IX.10, 1051b 15–25.

truths referred to in composite assertions from simple or unitary truths that are immediately known or unknown. The statement, for instance, that this house is uninhabited, can be true or false. Calling, in contrast, something a house, one does not attribute a kind of property to something, but rather grasps it as itself. Not grasping it is tantamount to missing it completely. In the case of the being-ness of a being, one cannot be wrong, only ignorant. Someone calling a house 'a ship' does not thereby err, but shows ignorance.

The distinction Aristotle draws is basically plausible. If nothing were stable and identical, it would not be possible to attribute properties or states to anything at all. That which is stable and identical is, however, true in a different way from something undergoing change. Whereas the latter, indeed, can be truly what it is only in different ways – like a bare-branched and foliate tree – and accordingly be discovered truly only in convictions and assertions affirming its particular state, the former – for instance a tree – is constantly what it truly is as long as it is. According to Aristotle, its truth is that of the full and constant actuality of its essential eidetic determination. Entire actuality is entirely and thus truly knowable.

This will differ from the foregoing critical revision of Aristotle's conception. If being-ness is conceived as horizontally determined potentiality, the truth of being-ness can no longer be entirely knowable. In grasping the being-ness of a house as its habitability, for example, one will immediately know what a building one views is. However, one will not know it entirely since habitability can be realized in many different and yet undiscovered ways. Though the essential possibility of a house indicated by an expression like 'habitability' will be immediately known by someone having an intuitive understanding of habitation, this knowledge will remain open for exploration, explanation, and exemplification. So whereas the immediate grasping of an Aristotelian being-ness is immediately fulfilled, the immediate grasping of a being-ness that has the character of an eidetic horizon is like a promise. A range of diverse possibilities is opened up that, with the immediate knowledge of a being-ness, motivates exploration.

In accordance with the designated character of being-ness, its truth must be different from that of an Aristotelian being-ness. Though also being a truth to be grasped immediately and intuitively, it is not a complete and ultimate presence in contrast to which the composite truths of something having properties or being in a particular state are only provisional. Rather, it is truth to be complemented by provisional truths – truth as an open potential that becomes explicit in particular possibilities. As explications of a particular horizontal truth these possibilities must also be true, though in another way. So with being-ness defined as eidetic horizon, truth, indeed, proves to be twofold – not, as Aristotle would say, one truth differentiated into an accomplished and a provisional version, but truth divided into two different truths complementing each other.

For an answer to the question of how this twofold truth can be conceived in detail, it will be helpful to discuss Heidegger's conception of truth as elaborated in his essay *On the Essence of Truth* (*Vom Wesen der Wahrheit*).[116]

---

[116] Martin Heidegger, Vom Wesen der Wahrheit, in: Weg-

In this essay, Heidegger most clearly explains a conception of truth already dominant in his Marburg lecture courses, especially in *Logic. The Question of Truth* (*Logik. Die Frage nach der Wahrheit*) and, of course, in the pertinent sections of *Being and Time*. For Heidegger's conception, the doubling of truth is programmatic.[117] Insofar Heidegger's essay can provide a conceptual frame for investigating how twofold truth could be conceived.

Heidegger begins his attempt to clarify the 'essence of truth' by discussing what he calls "the usual concept of truth" ("*der geläufige Begriff der Wahrheit*").[118] What he thereby means is what was previously discussed as the correlational meaning of the expression 'true', according to which the expression indicates something that appears as what it is – Heidegger's example is "true gold" as opposed to something that only seems to be gold – as well as convictions and statements referring to something as being true. Heidegger does not discuss convictions, but only statements characterizing those of them as true that are "in accordance" ("*in der Übereinstimmung*") with

---

marken, Gesamtausgabe vol. 9, ed. by Friedrich-Wilhelm von Herrmann, Frankfurt am Main 1976, 177–202. Quotations will be from an English translation by John Sallis, published in: Martin Heidegger, On the Essence of Truth, trans. by John Sallis, in: Basic Writings, edited by David Farrell Krell, revised and expanded edition, Abington UK/New York 1993, 115–138. References in the following will only be to this fourth version of the text. The foregoing versions, less elaborate and more tentative than the fourth one, are published in: Martin Heidegger, Vorträge, Teil I: 1915–1932, Gesamtausgabe vol. 80.1, ed. by Günther Neumann, Frankfurt am Main 2016, 327–428.

117 Cf. John Sallis, Double Truth, Albany N.Y. 1995.

118 Heidegger, Vom Wesen der Wahrheit, GA 9, 178; Heidegger, On the Essence of Truth, 116.

their correlate of reference.[119] Heidegger explains this accordance that he regards as characteristic for the "usual concept of truth" as "the consonance ("*Einstimmigkeit*") of a matter with what is supposed in advance regarding it and, on the other hand, the accordance of what is meant in the statement with the matter." One has, for instance, supposed that a coin lying on the table, is gold, and it proves to be gold. Thus, the statement that it is a golden coin is 'consonant' with the coin one refers to.

According to Heidegger, the double consonance just explained can also be conceived as "correctness" ("*Richtigkeit*"). This term allows Heidegger to designate different aspects of the 'usual concept of truth' with expressions derived from the same root. In languages other than German, this method can only be reproduced approximately. To this effect, one could say that a 'correct' statement is 'directed' to the subject matter it states, whereas this subject matter, being truly what it is, is 'directed' to the statement that lets its truth become obvious.

Despite these explications, however, it may still be unclear how the correlation of truth, indicated by the expressions 'accordance' ('*Übereinstimmung*'), 'consonance' ('*Einstimmigkeit*') and 'correctness' ('*Richtigkeit*') as such is to be conceived. Heidegger's expressions could be suspected of being sheer metaphors without descriptive force. Admittedly, they indicate a certain kind of person's referential experience according to which statements and subject matters fit together – what is stated really is the

---

[119] HEIDEGGER, Vom Wesen der Wahrheit, GA 9, 180: "die Einstimmigkeit einer Sache mit dem über sie Vorgemeinten und zum anderen die Übereinstimmung des in der Aussage Gemeinten mit der Sache"; HEIDEGGER, On the Essence of Truth, 117.

case, and what is the case becomes explicit in a statement. However, what needs clarification is the correlation. How is it experienced, and how is it possible? Attempting to answer these questions, Heidegger introduces the conception of truth he wishes to argue for, and in doing so reveals how he understands 'the essence of truth'.

The respective passage[120] in Heidegger's essay is conceptually dense and difficult to translate. Heidegger refers to the experience of appearance by attempting to uncover what could be called a 'primordial' relatedness that, as it were, underlies the 'normal' reference to something as it is performed in statements. In order for such a statement to be possible, something must be objectified – Heidegger's word is '*vor-stellen*', the literal meaning of which is approximately 'to set forward' – so that it can 'stand opposed' ("*Entgegenstehen*") and thus appear. Such appearance, however, is only possible within an openness that is not created by objectifying something, but rather "only entered into and taken over as a domain of relatedness" ("*nur als ein Bezugsbereich bezogen und übernommen*").

Heidegger's consideration just sketched could easily be taken as a description of spatial experience. What he calls '*vor-stellen*' is a kind of distancing oneself from something that, being distant, appears as an object or, to use the corresponding German expression, as *Gegenstand*, a word originally translated from the Latin word *oppositio* and thus designates the opposed positions of two planets.[121]

---

120 Heidegger, Vom Wesen der Wahrheit, GA 9, 184; Heidegger, On the Essence of Truth, 121.

121 Figal, Gegenständlichkeit.

Stressing that such an objectification needs an 'openness' in which it can take place, Heidegger seems to refer to space and especially to spatial expanse as the enabling of the 'primordial' correlation he attempts to reveal. This, however, is not the case. Speaking of the 'primordial' as standing "open to beings" – the German word is "*offenständig*" –[122] Heidegger implicitly introduces his conception of essential truth that he then makes explicit in two steps. He first explains the reference standing open to beings as grounded in *freedom*, understood as engagement "with the open region and its openness into which every being comes to stand."[123] And secondly, he determines the openness mentioned here as truth, understood as ἀλήθεια that, again, is translated as unconcealment (*Unverborgenheit*). So whereas freedom is to prove as the enabling of standing open to beings and thereby also as the objectification as a necessary condition for correctness, unconcealment – the essential truth – is supposed to enable freedom. As Heidegger says, "freedom is the ground of the inner possibility of correctness only because it receives its own essence from the more original essence of uniquely essential truth."[124]

---

[122] HEIDEGGER, Vom Wesen der Wahrheit, GA 9, 184; HEIDEGGER, On the Essence of Truth, 122.

[123] HEIDEGGER, Vom Wesen der Wahrheit, GA 9, 188: "sich einlassen auf das Offene und dessen Offenheit, in die jegliches Seiende hereinsteht"; On the Essence of Truth, 125.

[124] Heidegger, Vom Wesen der Wahrheit, GA 9, 187: "die Freiheit ist nur deshalb der Grund der inneren Möglichkeit der Richtigkeit, weil sie ihr eigenes Wesen aus dem ursprünglicheren Wesen der einzig wesentlichen Wahrheit empfängt"; On the Essence of Truth, 124–125.

In order to explicate this consideration, it may first be appropriate to comment on Heidegger's notion of freedom, which is not as puzzling as it may initially appear.[125] Characterizing freedom as engagement with openness or, in the same sense, as "letting be" ("*Seinlassen*"),[126] Heidegger does not evoke a kind of basic passivity, which could hardly be made intelligible as freedom. Rather, he indicates that in order to stand 'open to beings' a basic evidence of openness is required – just as one cannot experience something as 'over there', at a certain distance, without having an essential sense of space. Understanding such a sense of openness as freedom is by no means inadequate. Freedom to act, likely the most familiar kind of freedom, is also a sense of openness. In order to decide on a particular possibility to act, one must intuitively know or sense that nothing is yet decided and regard different options as possibilities that are left open. Freedom to act, again, requires a sense of the openness of everything that may be of whatever importance for one's possible actions, and, accordingly, the engagement with openness Heidegger speaks about includes freedom to act as only a particular version of freedom.

So far, however, freedom as Heidegger understands it has only partly been explicated. As a sense of openness, freedom is not possible without openness as such, provided that it cannot be regarded as its own openness. Heidegger implicitly excludes this by understanding freedom as 'engagement' with openness and stating that

---

125 Cf. Günter Figal, Martin Heidegger. Phänomenologie der Freiheit, 4th revised edition, Tübingen 2013.

126 Heidegger, Vom Wesen der Wahrheit, GA 9, 188; Heidegger, On the Essence of Truth, 125.

freedom "receives its own essence from the more original essence of uniquely essential truth." Truth enables freedom, and is thus 'more original' ('*ursprünglicher*') than freedom. It is 'uniquely essential' ('*einzig wesentlich*'), i.e., the only 'essence' possible. These characterizations are enigmatic – how should something be 'more original' instead of just being 'original', and how could truth be 'uniquely essential' if something else, namely freedom, also can be called 'essential'? The enigma may indicate that Heidegger's argument is not sound. Designating the 'essential truth' as 'more original', he implicitly characterizes freedom as 'original' – and how could something 'original' originate from something else?

The enigma can be unraveled if one is attentive to how Heidegger relates correctness, freedom, and the 'essential' truth to each other. Freedom, as it were, mediates between correctness and 'essential' truth, and there is good reason to assume that without this mediation the openness that freedom is engaged with could not be declared as 'truth' at all.

Freedom as Heidegger characterizes it enables a clear view of what there is, because in freedom one lets beings be and thus allows reference to beings as to what they truly are. Heidegger stresses this character of freedom, saying that an engagement "with the disclosedness of beings is not to lose oneself in them: rather, such engagement withdraws in the face of beings in order that they might reveal themselves with respect to what and how they are, and in order that presentative correspondence might take its standard from them."[127] Freedom is there-

---

[127] Heidegger, Vom Wesen der Wahrheit, GA 9, 188–189:

fore unbiased openness to beings and thus an engagement with truth. It allows correct statements for whose correctness the criterion is a being as 'standard' ('*Richtmaß*').

So far, the argument is sound but incomplete. The openness that freedom is is an engagement that could be characterized in more detail, although this would contribute nothing decisive to clarifying the 'possibility of correctness'. For this possibility, however, the openness of freedom – the openness that freedom is engaged with as well as the openness freedom is as such – is only a necessary and not a sufficient condition. What is instead required is an answer to the question of how beings can function as a standard for the correctness of convictions and statements. How can one know "what and how they are"?

Heidegger has no answer to this question. He only pretends to by designating the openness of freedom as truth and suggesting that correctness as such can be sufficiently explained by thinking "it back to that still uncomprehended disclosedness and disclosure of beings."[128] Heidegger simply projects the character of truth onto the openness essential for freedom, taking freedom as medi-

---

"Das Sicheinlassen auf die Entborgenheit des Seienden verliert sich nicht in dieser, sondern entfaltet sich in einem Zurücktreten von dem Seienden, damit dieses in dem, was es ist und wie es ist, sich offenbare und die vorstellende Angleichung aus ihm das Richtmaß nehme"; HEIDEGGER, On the Essence of Truth, 125.

[128] HEIDEGGER, Vom Wesen der Wahrheit, GA 9, 188: "den gewohnten Begriff der Wahrheit im Sinne der Richtigkeit der Aussage um- und zurückzudenken in jenes noch Unbegriffene der Entborgenheit und Entbergung des Seienden"; HEIDEGGER, On the Essence of Truth, 125.

ating between truth, understood as correctness, and the openness of being. He seems to assume that, if freedom is the essence of truth understood as correctness, then the essence of freedom must be the essence of truth.

Heidegger probably does so because he regards philosophy as devoted to the disclosing of being and wishes philosophy to be an engagement with truth as it has been since Parmenides. Heidegger's understanding of philosophical truth, however, contrasts starkly with what he previously stated in his essay about truth. The experience of the "truth of being as a whole" ("*Wahrheit des Seienden im Ganzen*")[129] is as such "the exposure to the disclosedness of beings as such" ("*die Aus-setzung in die Entborgenheit des Seienden als eines solchen*") resulting in the question, "what beings are" ("*was das Seiende sei*"), *nota bene* not "a particular sphere of beings" ("*ein besonderes Gebiet des Seienden*"), but rather "beings as such as a whole" ("*das Seiende als solches im Ganzen*").[130] This experience, however, is incompatible with freedom that, as an unbiased openness to beings, enables correctness. Heidegger himself makes this explicit saying that "precisely because letting be always lets beings be in a particular comportment and thus discloses them, it conceals beings as a whole."[131] How, then, should truth, understood as correctness be founded in "uniquely essential truth"?

---

129 Heidegger, Vom Wesen der Wahrheit, GA 9, 199; Heidegger, On the Essence of Truth, 135.

130 Heidegger, Vom Wesen der Wahrheit, GA 9, 189–190; On the Essence of Truth, 126.

131 Heidegger, Vom Wesen der Wahrheit, GA 9, 193: "Gerade indem das Seinlassen im einzelnen Verhalten je das Seiende sein läßt, zu dem es sich verhält, und es damit entbirgt, verbirgt es das Seiende im Ganzen"; Heidegger, On the Essence of Truth, 129–130.

Obviously, this essential truth has nothing whatsoever in common with the truth of particular beings.

This result is clearly unsatisfying. Explaining it, however, may show a way out of the problems of Heidegger's conception. Heidegger overstates the difference between the two versions of truth he discusses, and he does so not at least because he wishes to draw the line between an 'ontological' investigation of Being as such and 'ontic' explorations of beings as sharply as possible. And, to reiterate, in conceiving truth as unconcealment (ἀλήθεια) he wishes to determine a kind of truth that is the special preserve of philosophy. It was Heidegger himself, who, in his later years, regarded the latter endeavor as doomed to failure. In his essay *The End of Philosophy and the Task of Thinking* (*Das Ende der Philosophie und die Aufgabe des Denkens*), he strictly rejects the assumption that ἀλήθεια could be identified with 'truth'. Rather, as Heidegger says, Ἀλήθεια, understood as unconcealment, allows the possibility of truth and thus is 'not yet truth'.[132] This remark obliterates the argument of Heidegger's essay *On the Essence of Truth*.

Despite this result, one should not simply reject Heidegger's considerations concerning two different versions of truth. Especially if unconcealment is definitely not supposed to be truth, his considerations offer a perspective of how to understand truth in its twofold character and, accordingly, the twofold exploration of truth as it has been exposed at the beginning of these considerations.

---

[132] Martin Heidegger, Das Ende der Philosophie und die Aufgabe des Denkens, in: Zur Sache des Denkens, Gesamtausgabe vol. 14, ed. by Friedrich-Wilhelm von Herrmann, Frankfurt am Main 2007, 67–90, here 85–86.

In order to take up and revise Heidegger's distinction in such a way, it may be appropriate to start with a question Heidegger left unanswered, namely how truth as 'correctness' is enabled by another kind of truth that, with Heidegger, can be called 'essential'. The assumption of such an enabling is sound and can easily be made intelligible. Stating, to take up Heidegger's example that something is gold or, more precisely, made of gold, is only possible on the basis of a certain set of concepts and conceptual distinctions that very likely do not become explicit with a referential statement as such.[133] An expression like 'gold' can only be used meaningfully if one has an at least vague knowledge of gold as a metal of a certain appearance that can be distinguished from the appearance of other metals. Stating that something is made of gold thus implies, for instance, the assumption that it is not made of silver – which looks different – or of brass, which will also look slightly different at a closer view and have another weight. Thus, using the expression 'gold' and identifying something appearing as golden both belong to what can be called 'a conceptual horizon'. This horizon encompasses all concepts relevant for understanding an expression like 'gold' as well as appearances of something as gold in such a way that the mentioned expression can be relevant for their determination.

Such a determination, however, can only be appropriate if something determinable as such is determinate. Otherwise what pretends to be a determination would just be an arbitrary naming without any cognitive relevance. Being determinate in such a way that it can be re-

[133] Cf. Polanyi, The Tacit Dimension.

ferred to appropriately something appearing, then, must belong to the same conceptual horizon as the determining statement. Being encompassed by such a horizon, statements determining something conceptually can be appropriate, and appearances can be the determinacy of the appearing. A particular horizon, then, allows statements and appearances to be true and understood as a convergence of a statement and an appearance thus allows 'correctness'.

Encompassing both statements – and therefore convictions expressed in statements too – and appearances, a conceptual horizon is also 'eidetic', since eidetic determinations are such that they apply both to statements expressing convictions and appearances. Eidetic determinations allow convictions and statements as well as appearances to be true. Conjoining a statement with an appearance, they allow a statement to be an expression of knowledge and an appearance to be the self-revealing of something in a particular determinacy.

Such a conjuncture, however, is only allowed, and not guaranteed, because a particular eidetic determination is not isolated, but rather part of an eidetic horizon. So it does not as it were automatically determine a statement and an appearance. Something appearing, for instance, as gold in color, glittering, and hard is not necessarily an appearance of gold. It could also be made of brass and would thus have to be recognized as an appearance of a determinacy different from the one supposed. It was only, and falsely, believed to be gold because of its gold-colored, glittering, and hard appearance. In order to adjust one's belief, one would have to investigate the object in question more closely, and one could only do so on the basis of a sufficiently solid knowledge of what gold is. Such knowledge would be that of the eidetic determination 'gold' belonging to a particular eidetic horizon.

This result allows, at least in a first step, understanding the twofold character of truth. In order to understand a particular appearance as that of gold for instance, one must already have understood what gold is. This, again, is a kind of knowledge that, in the moment of identifying something as gold or made of gold, will normally remain, to use Polanyi's expression, 'tacit' or, as one can also say, alluding to the German title of Polanyi's book, 'implicit'. Nevertheless, this knowledge can be made explicit by explaining how the determination 'gold' belongs to a set or net of determinations – as a kind of metal that, because of its characteristic properties, can be distinguished from other metals like silver and brass. Such an explanation can be true or mistaken, and would accordingly reveal whether the tacit assumption that has led the designation of something as 'made of gold' is true knowledge or not. It is true knowledge only if the assumed position of the determination 'gold' in the set or net of determinations it belongs to is the position it truly has.

The tacit and explicable knowledge of gold is structurally different from the true conviction that something appearing is golden or made of gold. In case that it is true knowledge – and not only pretend knowledge – it is not true as in being 'correct'. It is not referential, and accordingly eidetic determinations are not correlates of knowledge and as such, as Plato's Socrates assumes in the *Republic*, beings. Rather, such knowledge is like that of grammatical structures. Usually such structures are performed in speaking and writing. However, they can also be made explicit, and thereby they become evident as possibilities of forming and performing meaningful sentences. Comparably, sets or nets of eidetic determinations are structures of reality as such and therefore possibilities of reference to what really is there. Alluding to a passage in Plato's *Philebus* already mentioned as anticipating Aristotle's definition of being-ness,[134] one also could say that they are 'within' real things as their immanent determinacy that can be made explicit in statements.

As a consequence of such an eidetic realism, eidetic determinations cannot be explored without reference to particularly appearing beings. Though, for instance, the eidetic determination of gold can be explained in the context of other metals, such an explanation would be void without appearing metals and especially appearing gold. Eidetic determinations need exemplification. The 'essential' truth of eidetic knowledge and the truth of 'correct' convictions and statements are interdependently related to each other. Correct reference to something as something is enabled by the 'essential' truth of eidetic determinations, which, conversely, is confirmed by true, i.e. 'correct' convictions and statements.

The objects appropriate for exemplifying eidetic determinations, for instance the determination of gold, can be rather unspecific. A small nugget of the metal may be sufficient for demonstrating what gold looks like, and it may even be more appropriate for this than a ring or a coin. Showing a ring or a coin may draw more attention to such a specific object than to the quality it has. Accordingly, for a demonstration of gold it may be helpful to

---

[134] PLATO, Philebus 16d.

show different objects of the same quality and thus make clear that not the specific form of an object or of different objects is meant, but only the specific quality. Mostly, however, and not by chance can such a quality only be demonstrated with particular objects. Viewing a vast plain from afar one may wonder whether it is water or sand, and in this case the quality in question would not be that of a particular object, but rather an 'amorphous quality', without shape and without visible limits.[135] Amorphous qualities are surely not the most prominent and important topics of explorations and experiences concerning truth, however. Though the question 'water or sand?' may be of practical importance, it is quite easy to answer, and once an answer has been found, there is nothing left to be found out. The same holds true for the question of whether something is made of gold or not. Admittedly, the investigation needed to ascertain this is somewhat more complex than in the case of 'sand or water'. However, what the two questions have in common is that they can be answered by deciding a simple alternative that, once adequately made, does not need or initiate any further investigation. In the case of the 'gold or not' question, this would be different if the alternative to be decided would be relevant for the valuation of a particular object like a ring or a coin. Whether such an object is gold or not will be of importance in regard to its origin or its value, and accordingly the 'gold or not' question does not refer to an isolated quality, but rather to a particular object that either has this quality or does not. Such quality, being factual or not, would belong to a multitude

---

[135] FIGAL, Unscheinbarkeit, 46–55.

of facts that contribute to the character of a particular object. Revealing such facts, one will discover the object they belong to, and in so doing, one will tacitly confirm Aristotle's assumption that the being of qualities, quantities, relations, and other characters of this kind is dependent on the being-ness of a being these characters are attributed to. Accordingly, the truth of such characters and of statements referring to them is dependent on the truth of being-ness and of its cognition.

The question of how the truth of being-ness can be experienced has already been touched upon. Given that being-ness is to be understood as eidetic horizon encompassing a being's possibilities, the truth of being-ness would be the accessibility of this eidetic horizon that, being accessible with a being can be touched and expressed immediately without any impairment. For instance, the being-ness of a house, its habitability, would immediately and intuitively be grasped as a horizon including particular possibilities of habitation that will not, however, become completely explicit with the encompassing possibility of a house to be inhabited. Likewise, a living being, say a cat, can be grasped as a cat in the 'first completion' of characteristic faculties without any detailed knowledge of particular possibilities of how a cat lives. An animal thus experienced will not only look like a cat, but can be recognized as a 'true cat' that has the potential to live as a cat by realizing possibilities at least partly explicit, and most certainly included in the eidetic horizon of 'cat-ness'. This horizon encompasses and thus defines the meaning of an animal as a cat.

Though the being-ness of a cat will be immediately evident to someone identifying a living being as a cat, the life potential of such an animal will not be intelligible without some examples of how a cat can or actually does live. Accordingly, the eidetic horizon of cat-ness can only be grasped with a real cat's behavior that, conversely, can only be identified as a cat's behavior since it is grounded in the potential of 'cat-ness'. So grasping the 'essential truth' of a cat's being-ness and 'correctly' identifying an animal's behavior as that of a cat, are reciprocally dependent on each other. The 'essential' truth of being-ness makes correctness possible, and itself needs confirmation by correctness.

Such a confirmation could be taken just as an exemplification of the kind illustrated by the example of gold. A closer look will reveal that in the case of being-ness, the confirmation is, however, different. Whereas an eidetic determination like that of gold is exhaustively exemplified with something of whatever kind provided that it is gold, a particular cat-like behavior of a cat will never exhaust the potential of cat-ness. Accordingly, grasping the cat-ness of a cat is a promise rather than a result – a motivation to find out more about the behavior of a cat and thus, again, to understand its life potential as enabling every particular cat-like behavior. The immediate evidence of cat-ness needs explication, and it can be explicated with possibilities and actualities of animal behavior that belong to the life potential of a cat and are as such distinctive – for instance, a particular way of moving that would be impossible for a dog or any other animal, or the ability to see in the dark. Such behavior would be 'correctly' ascribed to a cat, and this, again, is so because it would fit into the horizon of a cat's life potential or, to allude to Heidegger's essay on truth, would be *in accordance* with cat-ness. Such accordance, then, proves to be the criterion for particular convictions and statements referring to an animal's behavior as that of a true cat. They are true where the designated and described behavior truly is that of a cat or, to repeat, are in accordance with cat-ness.

It should be noted that not everything that can be said about a cat's behavior must be 'typical' or even specific for a cat. It can be as unspecific as the statement that a cat has four legs and a tail. This is nevertheless in accordance with what a cat as such is, and thus a correct statement. In its being-ness, however, a cat is more appropriately described with statements that capture something truly distinctive. Such statements are not only correct, but true explications of cat-ness as a particular being-ness. So on the one hand, the eidetic horizon of being-ness is *exclusive*. It excludes statements and the possibilities they refer to as not being in accordance with being-ness. Of this kind is the famous example Socrates gives for a false statement in Plato's *Sophist*: 'Theaetetus with whom I am speaking flies'.[136] This statement is not just false because the Eleatic stranger's interlocutor is actually sitting – which is correctly stated beforehand – and not flying around. Moreover, it is necessarily false because Theaetetus is a human being and as such is unable to fly – at least not without some technical equipment. On the other hand, the eidetic horizon of being-ness is *inclusive*: it includes every possibility that belongs to the particular potential of a being, regardless of whether it is a living being or a thing.

---

136 Plato, The Sophist 263a.

The example of a false statement from the *Sophist* just mentioned illustrates how the being-ness of something or someone can be paid various degrees of attention. Understanding the statement as false just because it asserts something that is not the case – Theaetetus is not flying, but sitting – one does not take into account that Theaetetus as a human being is unable to fly. Though Theaetetus is most likely understood as a human being, his human-ness remains just inconspicuous. Such a view only taking as relevant whether something is the case or not, is merely *empirical*. Realizing, however, that Theaetetus because of his human-ness is unable to fly unaided, one has become attentive to this human-ness and could thus take further steps to explore it. Such an exploration would make attempts to discover the attitudes and activities of a human being as indications of its specific possibilities and faculties and thus of its being-ness as its 'first completion'. What, from an empirical point of view, would be just facts, would now appear as a confirmation of a living being's potential to live, and also possibly as a surprising one irradiating this potential in a way unknown before. The characteristic faculties of a living being would then appear in a new light or even prove to be new faculties.

Such an exploration of being-ness can possibly best be illustrated with Aristotle's favorite example of architecture because it represents the whole process covering the intuitive knowledge of being-ness, more precisely the being-ness of a house, as well as the knowledge of how to realize this being-ness in a particular being. Thus, the example is paradigmatic for understanding the truth of architectural knowledge as truth of the particular being-ness architecture is concerned with, and also as truth becoming manifest with the accordance of a particular being with its being-ness. With an example like architecture, the convergence of 'subjective' and 'objective' truth is especially evident since the knowledge supposed to be true is not only that of a statement. Rather, it is a specific kind of 'knowing how', namely productive knowledge with which the 'objective' truth of what is known simultaneously becomes manifest with the truth of knowledge. The accomplishment of truth as a confirmation of 'essential' truth by accordance thus also becomes intelligible.

Intuitively grasping the being-ness of a house as its habitability, architects will by and large have an elaborate understanding of what is required for habitation in a variety of different social or cultural conditions. In any case, however, the being-ness of a house does not prescribe its individual particularities. Though nothing will be regarded as a house that cannot be understood within the eidetic horizon of a house's being-ness, the particular character of a house will not be predetermined, but is instead the result of design and building.

Depending on an architect's skill this result will be more or less schematic. In the case of architecture, routinely designed and built houses will all basically look alike and be similarly habitable. Architects, who are real artists, however, will understand every new project as a fresh challenge. They will endeavor to find a solution appropriate for a specific site as well as particular requirements of habitation. The being-ness of a house will thus be concretized in a particular building that, when successful, discovers habitability anew. With a house that is evidently a work of architectural art, habitability is brought to appearance – it appears with the appearance of the house as an appearance of how habitability can be. Such a house is a being in accordance with its being-ness and thus a true being of its kind – a true house.

Though houses of major quality are normally designed and built in accord with particular requirements of habitation, they cannot be reduced to such requirements – as if a house could be completely absorbed by the life of its inhabitants. Admittedly, the inhabitants of a house would recognize its 'objective meaning' of habitability, which is the being-ness of the house. But this meaning could not be a house's being-ness if only those who understand it could define it. That would render it merely 'subjective'. The 'objective meaning' of something like a house, to use a slightly paradox expression, can be 'more subjective' and 'more objective' so that an 'objective meaning' could be 'subjective objective' or 'objective objective', and both to varying degrees. A house, to explain this, could be 'subjectively' understood as convenient for habitation and thus appear as being made for its inhabitants. But a house could also be 'objectively' understood as disclosing what habitability and thus habitation can be and thus challenge its inhabitant's understanding of a house and of how to reside. With such an 'objective' view, a house is more or less explicitly understood in its being-ness as an appearance augmented by its eidetic horizon.

As a consequence of these considerations, the work of an architect could be designated as a kind of *mediation* between the being-ness of the product specific to architecture and certain conditions that include a particular situation as well as particular, more or less vague expectations of how this being-ness should be realized as the 'objective meaning' of a particular product. What the users of a product have 'between' being-ness and certain expectations is the product itself. The product is supposed to fulfill these expectations but to appear as what it is in accordance with the potential of its being-ness at the same time. Since a particular house will never just fulfill the expectations of possible inhabitants, but rather appear as being by itself, its 'objective objective meaning' precedes how its 'objective meaning' is subjectively conceived. It is an 'objective' being that allows the understanding of being-ness as such, either as something to be produced or as a being to be experienced, and insofar as 'subjective' conceptions are only valid if they are in accordance with an 'objective' being. For production as exemplified with architecture, the expectations of possible inhabitants cannot be a measure but only a particular condition that can – and mostly should – be taken into account. The measure is habitability as objectified in such a way that an 'object', a house, can be objectified habitability and thus be habitable. In this regard, the productive process of designing and building is not really a mediation, but rather an *application* – the realization of an objective meaning as the meaning of a particular object or, more precisely, of an object-like being like a house, under certain conditions.

'Application' is mainly a *hermeneutical* term.[137] It designates the explication of a meaning, mostly fixed as that of a text, under particular conditions that is led by the intention to demonstrate the meaning's appropriateness for these conditions. In this hermeneutical sense a law can be applied to a particular criminal case by adjudication, a

[137] Cf. Hans-Georg Gadamer, Wahrheit und Methode. Grundzüge einer philosophischen Hermeneutik. Hermeneutik I, Gesammelte Werke vol. 1, Tübingen 1986, 312–346.

biblical text to a congregation in a sermon or, in general, a text that needs explaining through its explication to a particular group. If this can be applied to architecture – and thereby also to productive skills of a comparable kind in general – then the architect's designing and, even more so, accomplishing a house is an application. With a house, habitability is 'applied' to a particular situation and thus made intelligible in a particular and specific way. Architecture, thus understood, is not only production, not to mention 'creation', but also and mainly recognition – more precisely, the recognition of the being-ness of a house in the process of designing and building. A particular being-ness initially grasped is explicated in the production of something that is in accordance with this being-ness and lets it become intelligible with its appearance. Insofar as this recognition has the character of application, the recognition of a particular being-ness is a hermeneutic process.

Also, living or sojourning in a house can be recognition of a comparable kind, provided, however, that the experience of habitability is not 'subjectively' centered and thus absorbed by personal habitation, but rather the experience of an 'objective objective meaning'. Then one's personal experience may reveal what habitability can be as that of a particular house. One allows the habitability of a house to be 'applied' to one's own habitation – like a reader of a text allows the text to be 'applied' to their capacity for understanding. An example of this kind is cognitive experience that reveals the potential of something in reference to its particular possibilities and actualities under the particular conditions of the experiencing person. It is like a reading of a text that is determined by a reader's capacity for understanding, referring to particular passages of a text and, being led by an intuitive grasping of the horizon of the text's meaning, attempting to understand this meaning explicitly. In doing so, one will more or less be explicitly aware of the fact that no reading will exhaust this meaning though, being a reading at all, will also never miss it completely. Being-ness is like a text and notwithstanding this, essentially different. It is not as clearly tied to the appearance of a particular being, as the meaning of a text is to the fixed structure of writing. A text is ultimately what it is, and though in a particular reading its meaning will not be understood completely, its intelligible structure is completely on the surface. In contrast to this, every being-ness as meaning is a potential that with every activity of a living being and every discovery of how something appears as 'usable', resurfaces partly anew. Despite this difference, however, the exploration of being-ness once intuitively grasped is a hermeneutical experience, an endeavor to recognize and explicate beings as the specific beings they truly are.

As already stressed, such an exploration of being-ness is only possible in reference to particular beings. As appearances, however, beings cannot be reduced to the potential that enables them to be what they are. Beings are not only intelligible, but also perceivable. Their perceptibility, however, may be dominated and almost absorbed by their intelligibility so that something viewed at first glance will be instantly recognized or taken as recognizable. Though dominated by intelligibility, however, the perceptibility of beings will not necessarily be neglected. It can also be regarded as a necessary condition for intelligibility or even as including a being's eidetic determinacy, so that not only the primary visible qualities of something can be seen, but also its 'categorical' determinations – not only the white color of a sheet of paper but also its rectangular shape. Husserl was first to describe such a perception of immediate epistemic relevance and designated it as 'categorical intuition' ('*kategoriale Anschauung*').[138]

Husserl's discovery is of such epistemological importance that it cannot be overestimated. How should it be possible to verify a statement according to which an object lying on the desk is a rectangular white sheet of paper without a possibility to see what is lying there, the qualities characteristic for paper included? And so, perception is not only a necessary condition, but immediately relevant for the experience of truth.

On the other hand, however, perception is not necessarily an epistemic experience, and accordingly the perceptible is not necessarily experienced as something being truly what it is. Perceiving something, one may have no idea what it could be nor the ambition to find out. The ambiguous object Valéry's Socrates is so much disconcerted by could just be viewed without epistemic intentions – without questioning what it is and how true statements about it would be possible. Rather, one could contemplate and also describe such an object – without doubting that it *is*, but also without any pronounced interest in its being. One would thus take something undoubtedly being just as appearance – as it were without any ontic augmentation, not primarily, or even not at all

---

[138] Cf. HUSSERL, Logische Untersuchungen II.2, Husserliana XIX.2, 657–691; cf. FIGAL, Unscheinbarkeit, 268–278.

appearing as an eidetic determinate. For such contemplation, accordingly, the question of truth would lose its importance. Contemplating an ambiguous object or something as an ambiguous object would therefore lead beyond being and truth – beyond metaphysics.

VIII. Beyond Metaphysics

Transcending metaphysics must not be confused with the historical project initiated by Nietzsche and so effectively pursued by Heidegger. Metaphysics as conceived in the foregoing considerations is not the epoch of philosophy beginning with Parmenides and ending with Hegel that, following Derrida, could be regarded as 'closed' in favor of a 'non-metaphysical' or 'post-metaphysical' thinking of whatever kind.[139] If, as has been shown, metaphysics is philosophy concerned with truth and, as a consequence, also with being, then it is a philosophical endeavor that cannot be overcome without abandoning the question of truth as such. This, however, would be tantamount to doubting the very possibility of knowledge and thus of a human life led in accordance with the objective world. However, the objects and facts of this world really are accessible, and the capacity to pursue one's aims amid experienced objects and other living beings is neither an illusion nor a result of subjective sovereignty.

Maintaining the metaphysical quest for truth and hence the quest for a clarification of being, one should, however, be especially attentive to topics that are not to be integrated into a metaphysical perspective. As touched on already, these are topics concerning the primordial, preliminarily explained as appearance that is

---

[139] Jacques Derrida, De la grammatologie, Paris 1967.

not contrasted to being as such, but rather to being insofar as it is distinctly determined by being-ness and other eidetic determinations. Questioning the primordial is metaphysically necessary where eidetic determinations do not constitute being as such, but rather augment it. Since being, then, cannot be reduced to eidetic determinations, its phenomenal character has to be taken into account to ensure an adequate and thorough investigation of being.

Such an investigation as outlined earlier could be regarded as a completion of metaphysical philosophy. Devoted to 'the other side of being' it would be an integral part of metaphysical investigations. This, however, is not the case, since the primordial is not being in a metaphysical sense and thus not subordinate to the metaphysical quest for truth. It is not a 'mere appearance' that could be contrasted to a 'real', i.e., really determinate being, but 'just appearance'. Accordingly, it is experienced as appearing without any attempt to determine and state, what it is. Nevertheless, the primordial is not purely indefinite in a way that one would be unable to describe it. It is not nothing, but something that, like Valéry's ambiguous object, may have a particular shape and surface, is of a certain size and weight, and is by all means determinate. However, one will fall short of its specific determinacy by attempting to grasp it in a web of distinct determinations. For instance, a surface of water glittering in the sunlight and gently rippling in the wind will be recognized instantly and nevertheless remain inexhaustible through any attempt at determination. Someone contemplating such a surface will mostly regard such an attempt as pointless. Why should one try to distinguish the water's innumerable shades of blue or to count the ever-changing reflections of light? Obviously, such a surface of water is adequately experienced without such attempts, and is accordingly nothing that lends itself to a metaphysical ambition of knowledge and truth. It is not conceivable in its being-ness; opinions and statements cannot grasp it, and as a result one cannot fail to recognize it adequately either.

The example just given is appropriate for explaining the primordial in two further respects. First, the example does not only exemplify the innumerably varying quality of something primordial, but thereby also the irreducibility of its appearance. Since something primordial is as such eidetically undetermined, it will not appear to someone as prefigured by presuppositions of what it in particular is. Though a surface of water can easily be identified, this knowledge is not really relevant for the experience of its glittering and the variety of its colors. Subsequently, its recognizability as water will not open up a field of possible questions concerning the specific character of water and motivate further investigation. Instead, the glittering variety of its colors will simply be taken as the appearance that it is. One will just face it as it comes into view, without presuppositions or specific expectations.

Experiencing a body of water, one will, secondly, not primarily be attentive to the particular form before one. It will be insignificant whether this body of water is a lake, a river, or the open sea. Attending to just the water's surface, one will experience an extension the limits of which are irrelevant – and can be so because extension as such is unlimited.

The primordial, to recap, is indefinite variety and thus *inexhaustible*, it appears immediately and is thus *encountered*, without limits, allowing limitation, but essentially being *beyond* it. In these three respects, the primordial is in contrast to being conceived metaphysically, which is essentially determinate so that it can be definitely known as a limited form.

The contrast of the primordial with being as it is metaphysically conceived implicitly or explicitly dominates metaphysical philosophy from the very beginning. Parmenides, though tacitly, excludes the primordial from philosophy, stressing the determinacy of beings as well as of knowledge devoted to it, and, most notably, conceiving the totality of being as a limited whole. As can be read in Parmenides' poem, "strong Necessity holds" being "within the bonds of a limit, which keeps it on ever side" and "since there is a furthest limit," being is "perfected" so that it can be compared to "the bulk of a bowl well-rounded on ever side."[140] Plato, contrary to Parmenides, does not exclude the primordial, but rather offers a dense and enigmatic discussion of it in the *Timaeus*, introducing 'land' (χώρα) as the indefinite ground and receptacle for definite forms.[141] Aristotle finally adopts Plato's discussion of χώρα and transforms it into his own conception of 'matter'.

---

140 Parmenides, VS, B 8, 30–31: κρατερὴ γὰρ Ἀνάγκη/πείρατος ἐν δεσμοῖσιν ἔχει, τό μιν ἀμφίς ἐέργει; B 8, 42–43: αὐτάρ ἐπεὶ πεῖρας πύματον, τετελεσμένον ἐστί/πάντοθεν, εὐκύκλου σφαίρης ἐναλίγκιον ὄγκωι.

141 For an extensive discussion of χώρα cf. Figal, Unscheinbarkeit, 38–56.

However, Plato's and Aristotle's considerations, though crucial for their respective conceptions of how eidetic determinations can appear, are not their main philosophical concern. As pointed out earlier, both are mainly interested in how the question of truth can be answered in a conception of being as something entirely knowable. But it is worth noting that this metaphysical program of philosophy does not entirely exclude and barely marginalizes the primordial so that it would have to be rediscovered – and could possibly only be rediscovered in overcoming metaphysics. If metaphysics can be complemented by philosophical conceptions discovering aspects of the primordial that cannot, or can only insufficiently be taken into account metaphysically, then there is no need to overcome metaphysics at all.

Such philosophical conceptions have already been developed or at least touched upon in metaphysical contexts. Such is the inexhaustible abundance of appearance introduced with considerations on the beautiful as the correlate of 'true pleasure' in Plato's *Philebus*;[142] encounter as immediate experience irreducible to knowledge is presented dramatically in Plato's dialogues whenever individuals face others – in discussing philosophical topics face-to-face, something radically different from the topics discussed is experienced; and, finally, beyond the limits of a world comparable to a well-rounded bowl, comes not only χώρα as it is discussed in the *Timaeus*, but also the 'idea of the good', which, according to the *Republic*, enables truth as well as being-ness and thus is 'beyond

142 Plato, Philebus 51b.

being-ness', ἐπέκεινα τῆς οὐσίας.[143] To introduce terms that designate the philosophical conceptions related to these topics, one could speak of an *aesthetical*, an *ethical*, and a *mystical* aspect of the primordial. Accordingly, aesthetics, ethics, and mysticism could be regarded as philosophical endeavors transcending metaphysics.

Such a use of the terms just introduced does not presuppose philosophical aesthetics, ethics, and mysticism – after all, their belonging to philosophy might be doubted – as homogenous disciplines that are exclusively devoted to aspects of the primordial. There are, however, good reasons to assume that philosophical discussions of the beautiful cannot easily be subordinated to the metaphysical question of truth and being. It is not accidental that the attempt to do this by understanding art as a manifestation of truth may go along with a critical rejection of aesthetics.[144]

On the same strength, ethics, howsoever its particular versions may differ from each other, is not centered on metaphysical topics. Even Aristotle, referring in the *Nicomachean Ethics* to the structure of the human soul and thus to the being-ness of human beings, does not regard being-ness as the main topic of ethical discourse. His reference is quite brief, and the reason quite obvious. Ethical discourse is not primarily addressed to philosophers investigating the essence or 'nature' of human beings, but rather to the citizens of a *polis* seeking to live a good life. Ethics is hence mainly about practice, including the

---

143 Plato, The Republic 509b.

144 Cf. Figal, Erscheinungsdinge, 33–52.

practice of philosophy, which, ethically speaking, is not regarded as leading to insight, but rather to full happiness that, as Aristotle says alluding to the idea of the good as it is discussed in the *Republic*, excels everything in its potential and dignity.[145] Kant in a way makes the same point by arguing that a 'pure', i.e., non-empirical and therein 'metaphysical' conception of practical reason, necessarily goes back to freedom that as such cannot be explained but has to be taken as a 'fact'. It is a fact beyond the 'theoretical use of reason' and thus of being, a fact only to be experienced with the performance of practical reason as such.[146]

As already mentioned, speaking of 'mysticism' with regard to philosophy may sound strange and inappropriate. However, the term is not meant to indicate 'spiritual' experience as it is performed in meditation or diverse kinds of ascetic practice. Such experience, though not necessarily obscure and 'irrational', certainly would be beyond philosophy. The term is supposed to designate a specific experience with conceptual reference, more precisely the attempt not to stick to intelligible beings of whatever kind, rather than to transcend everything intelligible in order to 'touch' the ground of everything that as such is 'nothing' in the literal sense – no thing, no being. Meister Eckhart described such an intellectual move

---

[145] Aristotle, Nicomachean Ethics X.7, 1178a 1–2. Quotations are taken from: Aristotelis Ethica Nicomachea, ed. by Ingram Bywater, Oxford 1894.

[146] Immanuel Kant, Critique of Practical Reason, in: Practical Philosophy, trans. and ed. by Mary J. Gregor, Cambridge 1996, 133–172, 200 (A 74).

in his sermon on poverty as the only way to come close to God, who is neither being nor essence, but empty of all essence and only because of this can be all that is.[147] Such a mystic move, however, is not necessarily theological, but rather applies to every encompassment of being that is not being or being-ness and accordingly cannot be referred to in line with deictic gestures. Whereas one can point to something or someone, one cannot point to space that allows everything to appear. Though space as the enabling of appearance is experienced 'with' every appearance, it does not itself appear. Likewise, the world encompassing everything and everyone and thus made 'worldly' is not something one could refer to.

If the explanations offered here are sound, then aesthetics, ethics, and mysticism are indeed beyond metaphysics. Transcending being and being-ness and, accordingly, opinion and knowledge too, they are beyond truth. So not accidentally have aesthetical, ethical, and mystical arguments been produced in order to criticize or even overcome metaphysics.

This may, first, be illustrated with Nietzsche's attempt in *The Birth of Tragedy* to unmask Socrates, the paradigmatic metaphysical philosopher in Plato's dialogues, as a poet in disguise who is yet ignorant of the poetical character of his thinking.[148] As already mentioned, Nietzsche argued in later writings like *The Gay Science* that the "world that regards human beings" is not just

---

[147] Meister Eckhart, Sermon 52. Quoted from: Meister Eckhart, Werke in zwei Bänden, trans. by Josef Quint, ed. by Niklaus Largier, vol. 1, Frankfurt am Main 1993.

[148] Friedrich Nietzsche, Die Geburt der Tragödie, KSA 1, 9–156, here 81–102, sections 12–15.

recognized, but has been poetically invented by 'us' as the poets of life.[149]

As to ethics, Heidegger as author of *Being and Time* was the first to critically revise the 'metaphysical' question of being from a point of view adopted from Aristotle's conception of practical knowledge. Heidegger, however, though transcending ontology with his 'fundamental ontology', still pursues the metaphysical question of being and truth. It was Levinas who went a step further in claiming to ethically overcome the metaphysical commitment to being as such. As he argues, the 'epiphany' of the other's 'face' – the origin of ethics – transcends being, since it can neither be regarded as something to be known nor integrated into one's own sphere of being. It is, as Levinas says with Plato's phrase, beyond being, ἐπέκεινα τῆς οὐσίας.[150]

And it was Wittgenstein who prominently introduced mysticism as a critical position opposing metaphysics. In the final sections of his *Tractatus* he designates the "world" that, at the very beginning of the treatise, has been called "the totality of facts" as a "limited whole" and thus – very likely involuntarily – alludes to Parmenides' conception of the totality of being, resembling a 'well-rounded' bowl.[151] Presupposing that only statements on

---

149 Nietzsche, Die fröhliche Wissenschaft, KSA 3, 540, section 301.

150 Emmanuel Levinas, En découvrant l'existence avec Husserl et Heidegger, 4th edition, Paris 1982.

151 Ludwig Wittgenstein, Tractatus logico-philosophicus, kritische Edition, ed. by Brian McGuinness and Joachim Schulte, Frankfurt am Main 1989. English translation by C.K. Ogden, London 1955. Cf. Wittgenstein, Tractatus 6.45: "Die Anschauung der Welt sub specie aeternitati ist ihre Anschauung als begrenztes Gan-

facts have a meaning and that all statements or propositions "are of equal value,"[152] he concludes that statements on the world are meaningless. This, however, does not mean that speaking of 'the world' would be akin to uttering nonsense. Though meaningful statements about the world are supposed to be impossible, the world can be experienced. It can be "felt" and, as Wittgenstein explains, "the feeling of the world as a limited whole is the mystical feeling."[153] Given that meaningful statements about the world are impossible, such feeling cannot be linguistically articulated. So a mystical feeling will necessarily go along with silence; only with silence will it arise, whereas with attempts to speak about it, the feeling will fade away. Thus, the famous last sentence of the *Tractatus* – "whereof one cannot speak, thereof one must be silent"[154] – is a plea for the silence of mystical feeling and a rejection not only of speaking about 'the world', but in general about something that is not a fact, but rather a metaphysical topic like being-ness. One could certainly argue that in the *Tractatus* Wittgenstein himself does not only speak about facts, but about metaphysical topics like the world and, though it requires silence, about mystical feeling. Wittgenstein would counter this objection indicating the preliminary and therapeutic character of his text: "My propositions are elucidatory in this way: he

---

zes." WITTGENSTEIN, Tractatus 1.1: "Die Welt ist die Gesamtheit der Tatsachen, nicht der Dinge." Cf. FIGAL, Unscheinbarkeit.

[152] WITTGENSTEIN, Tractatus 6.4: "Alle Sätze sind gleichwertig."

[153] WITTGENSTEIN, Tractatus 6.45: "Das Gefühl der Welt als begrenztes Ganzes ist das mystische."

[154] WITTGENSTEIN, Tractatus 7: "Wovon man nicht sprechen kann, darüber muß man schweigen."

who understands me finally recognizes them as senseless, when he has climbed out through them, on them, over them. (He must so to speak throw away the ladder, after he has climbed up on it.)"[155]

Wittgenstein, as one may resume, reduces language to mere description in order to reserve every topic beyond facts to silent experience. He thus transforms metaphysics into mysticism, suspecting language beyond normal use as problematic – a suspicion he still entertains in his *Philosophical Investigations* explaining philosophizing as "confusion" that arises "when language is, as it were, idling, not when it is doing work."[156] Why, however, should philosophizing not also be possible as the linguistic work that Wittgenstein, with his own texts, confirms it to be? Though an expression like 'the world' admittedly does not refer to something being – what must be so since the world encompasses all beings – such a concept can meaningfully be used if related to expressions with reference to beings. Though statements about the world and other topics alike are neither true nor false since they do not refer to something, they can be meaningfully used *in relation* to true statements. So the mystical is not as isolated and locked in silence as Wittgenstein suggests. It can be mediated – and is always more or less explicitly mediated

---

[155] Wittgenstein, Tractatus 6.54: "Meine Sätze erläutern dadurch, daß sie der, welcher mich versteht, am Ende als unsinnig erkennt, wenn er durch sie – auf ihnen – über sie hinweggestiegen ist. (Er muß sozusagen die Leiter wegwerfen, nachdem er auf ihr hinaufgestiegen ist.)"

[156] Wittgenstein, Philosophische Untersuchungen/Philosophical Investigations, 132: "Die Verwirrungen, die uns beschäftigen, entstehen gleichsam, wenn die Sprache leerläuft, nicht wenn sie arbeitet."

whenever a mystical thought or feeling is experienced as meaningful. Only with such mediation can mysticism be philosophical.

This consideration can be generalized with regard to all philosophy beyond metaphysics. Maintaining the mystical character of the world, Wittgenstein disputes the possibility of descriptive philosophy – like Levinas who, discovering the originality of being faced by the other, doubts the credibility of ontology, and like Nietzsche who, discovering the creative or poetical side of philosophy, doubts its epistemological character. Though beyond metaphysics, however, aesthetics, ethics, and mysticism should not be regarded as better philosophical alternatives. There is no reason why philosophies investigating and discussing topics different from those of metaphysics should be superior to it. The argument according to which metaphysics 'forgets', 'ignores', or 'mistakes' something essential does not refute metaphysics *per se*. Why should metaphysics include every philosophical topic instead of being one particular perspective of philosophy? So the critique of metaphysis as exemplified with the arguments of Nietzsche, Levinas, and Wittgenstein tacitly presupposes metaphysical philosophy to include every topic and to solve every problem. This, however, is an overestimation of metaphysics, and this overestimation alone motivates its critique. Metaphysics is a limited philosophical project with a limited range of topics, questions, and answers. To be on the side of metaphysics, one should realize its limits.

This, however, also applies to philosophical endeavors beyond metaphysics, namely aesthetics, ethics, and mysticism. They are philosophical projects devoted to topics not to be integrated into metaphysical philosophy, and they also are limited in relation to each other. Their topics are different, as are the questions and answers they discuss. Though being limited and different from each other aesthetics, ethics, and mysticism are not isolated. They partially share topics and complement each other. The beautiful as the main topic of aesthetics has, for instance, been regarded as familiar with the good as the main topic of ethical thinking from Plato on, especially in the *Symposium* and the *Philebus*. In the *Republic* the 'idea of the good', a mystical idea that transcends metaphysics, is designated as the main content (μέγιστον μάθημα) of ethical thinking because it orients toward a good life. Kant restated the affinity between aesthetics and ethics by calling the beautiful 'a symbol of morality', and, finally, Hannah Arendt's last philosophical project was that of a political philosophy based on Kant's conception of aesthetical judgment.

The affinities between different ways of philosophy do not exclude metaphysics. Though aesthetics, ethics, and mysticism are not about being and being-ness they more or less explicitly or even tacitly rely on metaphysical questions. How should one discuss the very status of an artwork without reference to things like pictures that, as works of art, also are things and thus objects of metaphysical clarification? How should ethics discuss the very status of human activities without reference to the being-ness of persons performing actions? Or relate to things that are discovered, produced, or changed through actions? And, as already mentioned, how should mysticism explain its non-referential conceptions if not in relation to referential concepts that are a topic of epistemology and thus of metaphysics? Without taking being into account, all other philosophical endeavors would run the risk of becoming fiction. Such affinities will be more or less explicit in different philosophical conceptions. However, they will be there and by no means impair the original and particular character of the main philosophical projects.

'Metaphysics contextualized' – this idea can thus summarize the foregoing considerations, stressing again that the question of metaphysics is not that of a simple historical decision whether to maintain metaphysics or not. How should it even be possible to abolish it without at the same time doing without insight into a world dominated by the quest of knowledge and by science in a way that is unthinkable without Ancient Greek philosophy and thus without metaphysics? Heidegger's idea of transcending this world in favor of a 'new beginning' is, to say the least, not realistic. Seeking to understand a world of knowledge and science, we cannot do without metaphysics. However, this world cannot be exhausted by knowledge and science – it also has an aesthetical, an ethical, and a mystical dimension. Hence metaphysics is to be contextualized and thus to be regarded as one philosophical project among others. Contextualized metaphysics is less dramatic than metaphysics has been during the last two centuries. It has become or is about to become a normal philosophical project among others.

Bibliography

ARISTOTLE, Metaphysics. Quotations taken from: Aristotelis Metaphysica, ed. by W. D. Ross, 2 volumes, Oxford 1924.

–, Metaphysics. Translation quoted from: ARISTOTLE, Metaphysics, Books I–IX, with an English Translation by Hugh Tredennick, Cambridge Mass./London 1933.

–, Nicomachean Ethics. Quotations taken from: Aristotelis Ethica Nicomachea, ed. by Ingram Bywater, Oxford 1894.

–, Nicomachean Ethics. Translation quoted from: ARISTOTLE, The Nicomachean Ethics, with an English Translation by H. Rackham, Cambridge Mass./London 1926.

–, On the Soul. Quotations taken from: Aristotelis De anima, ed. by W. D. Ross, Oxford 1956.

–, Topics. Quotations taken from: Aristotelis Topica et Sophistici elenchi, ed. by W. D. Ross, Oxford 1958.

AUGUSTINE, Confessionum Libri XIII, Corpus Christianorum Series Latina XXVII, ed. by Lukas Verheijen, Turnholt 1981.

DERRIDA, JACQUES, De la grammatologie, Paris 1967.

FIGAL, GÜNTER, Ando. Raum, Architektur, Moderne, Freiburg 2017.

–, Erscheinungsdinge. Ästhetik als Phänomenologie, Tübingen 2010.

–, Finding the Right Concepts, in: FIGAL, Freiräume. Phänomenologie und Hermeneutik, Tübingen 2017, 71–81.

–, Gegenständlichkeit. Das Hermeneutische und die Philosophie, 2nd revised edition, Tübingen 2018.

–, Martin Heidegger. Phänomenologie der Freiheit, 4th revised edition, Tübingen 2013.

–, Unscheinbarkeit. Der Raum der Phänomenologie, Tübingen 2015.

GADAMER, HANS-GEORG, Wahrheit und Methode. Grundzüge einer philosophischen Hermeneutik. Hermeneutik I, Gesammelte Werke vol. 1, Tübingen 1986.

GOCLENIUS, RUDOLPH, Lexicon philosophicum, Frankfurt am Main 1613.

HEIDEGGER, MARTIN, Being and Time, trans. by Joan Stambaugh, New York 1996.

–, Das Ende der Philosophie und die Aufgabe des Denkens, in: Zur Sache des Denkens, Gesamtausgabe vol. 14, ed. by Friedrich-Wilhelm von Herrmann, Frankfurt am Main 2007, 67–90.

–, Grundprobleme der Phänomenologie, Gesamtausgabe vol. 24, ed. by Friedrich-Wilhelm von Herrmann, Frankfurt am Main 1975.

–, On the Essence of Truth, trans. by John Sallis, in: Basic Writings, ed. by David Farrell Krell, revised and expanded edition, Abington UK/New York 1993, 115–138.

–, Sein und Zeit, Gesamtausgabe vol. 2, ed. by Friedrich-Wilhelm von Herrmann, Frankfurt am Main 1976.

–, Vom Wesen der Wahrheit, in: Wegmarken, Gesamtausgabe vol. 9, ed. by Friedrich-Wilhelm von Herrmann, Frankfurt am Main 1976, 177–202.

–, Vorträge, Teil I: 1915–1932, Gesamtausgabe vol. 80.1, ed. by Günther Neumann, Frankfurt am Main 2016.

–, Einführung in die Metaphysik, Gesamtausgabe vol. 40, ed. by Petra Jaeger, Frankfurt am Main 1983.

HERACLITUS is quoted from: The Presocratic Philosophers. A Critical History with a Selection of Texts, ed. by G. S. Kirk, J. E. Raven, and M. Schofield, 2nd edition, Cambridge 1983.

HUSSERL, EDMUND, Erfahrung und Urteil. Untersuchungen zur Genealogie der Logik (1938), ed. by Ludwig Landgrebe, 7th edition, Hamburg 1999.

–, Erste Philosophie (1923/1924). Zweiter Teil. Theorie der phänomenologischen Reduktion, Husserliana VIII, ed. by Rudolf Boehm, The Hague 1959.

–, Ideen zu einer reinen Phänomenologie und phänomenologischen Philosophie. Erstes Buch. Allgemeine Einführung in die reine Phänomenologie, Husserliana III.1, ed. by Karl Schuhmann, The Hague 1976.

–, Logische Untersuchungen II.2, Husserliana XIX.2, ed. by Ursula Panzer, The Hague 1984.

–, Analysen zur passiven Synthesis. Aus Vorlesungs- und Forschungsmanuskripten 1918–1926, Husserliana XI, ed. by Margot Fleischer, The Hague 1966.

–, Cartesianische Meditationen, Husserliana I, ed. by Stephan Strasser, The Hague 1963.

KANT, IMMANUEL, Critique of Practical Reason, in: Practical Philosophy, trans. and ed. by Mary J. Gregor, Cambridge 1996, 133–272.

KIRKHAM, RICHARD L., Theories of Truth, Cambridge Mass. 1992.

LEVINAS, EMMANUEL, En découvrant l'existence avec Husserl et Heidegger, 4th edition, Paris 1982.

LIDDELL, HENRY GEORGE/SCOTT, ROBERT, A Greek-English Lexicon, Oxford 1951.

MEISTER ECKHART, Werke in zwei Bänden, trans. by Josef Quint, ed. by Niklaus Largier, vol. 1, Frankfurt am Main 1993.

NIETZSCHE, FRIEDRICH, Die fröhliche Wissenschaft, in: Sämtliche Werke, Kritische Studienausgabe, ed. by Giorgio Colli and Mazzino Montinari, vol. 3, Berlin/New York 1980, 342–552.

–, Die Geburt der Tragödie, in: Sämtliche Werke, Kritische Studienausgabe, ed. by Giorgio Colli and Mazzino Montinari, vol. 1, Berlin/New York 1980, 9–156.

–, Ueber Wahrheit und Lüge im aussermoralischen Sinne (1873), in: Sämtliche Werke, Kritische Studienausgabe, ed. by Giorgio Colli and Mazzino Montinari, vol. 1, Berlin/New York 1980, 875–897.

PARMENIDES is quoted from: The Presocratic Philosophers. A Critical History with a Selection of Texts, ed. by G. S. Kirk, J. E. Raven, and M. Schofield, 2nd edition, Cambridge 1983.

PLATO is quoted from: Platonis Opera, ed. by John Burnet, Oxford 1900–1907.
–, The Republic. Translation quoted from: PLATO, The Republic of Plato. Translated, with Notes, an Interpretative Essay, and a New Introduction by Allan Bloom, 2nd edition, New York 1991.
–, The Sophist. Translation quoted from: PLATO, Theaetetus, Sophist, with an English Translation by Harold North Fowler, Cambridge Mass./London 1921.
POLANYI, MICHAEL, The Tacit Dimension, New York 1966.
RYLE, GILBERT, The Concept of Mind, London/New York 1949.
SALLIS, JOHN, Double Truth, Albany N.Y. 1995.
STRAWSON, PETER F., Individuals. An Essay in Descriptive Metaphysics, London 1959.
TUGENDHAT, ERNST, TI KATA TINOΣ. Eine Untersuchung zu Struktur und Ursprung Aristotelischer Grundbegriffe, Freiburg/München 1958.
VALÉRY, PAUL, Eupalinos ou l'architecte, in: Œuvres, ed. by Jean Hytier, vol. 2, Paris 1960, 79–147.
WILLIAMS, BERNARD, Truth and Truthfulness. An Essay in Genealogy, Princeton/New Jersey/Oxford 2002.
WITTGENSTEIN, LUDWIG, Philosophical Investigations. The German text with an English translation by G.E.M. Anscombe, P.M.S. Hacker, and Joachim Schulte, 4th revised edition by P.M.S. Hacker and Joachim Schulte, London 2009.
–, Tractatus logico-philosophicus, kritische Edition, ed. by Brian McGuinness and Joachim Schulte, Frankfurt am Main 1989.
–, Tractatus logico-philosophicus, trans. by C.K. Ogden, London 1955.

List of Persons

---

* indicates mentionings in footnotes.